Mules In The Fast Lane

To my new friend, Cliff Davis - a fellow "mule" in the fast lane!

Best Wishes!

Mike Moody

3/4/19

Mules In The Fast Lane

Going Straight When Life Throws You a Curve...And Other Life Lessons from the Formative Years

Mike Moody

2005

Mules In The Fast Lane

CONTENTS

The roots of my raisin' run deep;
I've come back for the strength that I need.
And hope comes no matter how far down I sink;
The roots of my raisin' run deep.

—*Merle Haggard*

ACKNOWLEDGMENTS
AND
SPECIAL THANKS

To my beautiful daughters, Ashley and Crystal,
who have always had faith in me

To my sweet and precious granddaughter, Makayla
who entertained herself for countless hours at my house
while I worked on the manuscript

To my incredible sister, Jean,
who has protected me since Day One

To my parents, John and Lillie,
who, with the help of God, gave me life

To my friend and fellow counselor, Stephanie Calhoun,
who built a fire under me to start this book

And to the many unforgettable friends and family
who have cheered me on as I unlocked the doors
to my past and rediscovered them on the other side of my memory

My First Memory

Since becoming a Licensed Professional Counselor several years ago, I've used a technique to get my clients to "open up" and deal with possible unresolved issues of childhood that might be causing them psychological distress in the present. We've all heard of "repressed memories," and the jury is still out as to whether (1) there really is such a phenomenon, or (2) if there is, should we try to bring those memories back, or (3) if we do, will it serve any constructive purpose, or in fact do more harm than good?

So, a technique I use is First Memory Recollection. (By the way, this is not only a great therapeutic tool, but also a terrific ice-breaker at a party or social gathering as a way to get to know other people.) In my work, I have found that many people (probably 80 per cent or more) will relate a traumatic or painful event rather than a pleasurable experience as their first memory. For example, it will usually be something like, "I remember falling down the stairs," or "I think my father was spanking me." Rarely will the recollection be, "I remember my mother rocking me to sleep in her arms."

I don't remember my birth, of course, but the story has been told many times about how I got my name (and I've had to repeat it many times in explanation). My mother and father apparently couldn't decide on a name, and they weren't sure if I was to be a boy or girl, so they reportedly put several "possibilities" into a hat and drew it out sometime before my birth. My father's name was John William, so there were several names they thought would pair well with John. The name drawn was John Milton, and so it was to be. However, that name lasted only a few minutes, because, as the story goes, when the nurse brought me in to my mother shortly after my birth, she proudly (and erroneously) announced, "Well, here's little Mike!" And the rest is history. (The "little" part did prove to be true, however, because the rest of the story is told that I was so small—five pounds, nine ounces—my parents put me in a shoebox to show me off!) I've been explaining all my life how my "real" name is John Milton, but my "nickname" is Mike. I'm sure that nurse would be surprised if she knew the profound effect that simple utterance had on my life.

My family and I moved off the farm in 1947 when I was three years old after my father bought a run-down "Mom and Pop" store with gas pumps out front, aptly named "The Triangle," because of its location at the intersection of two well-known highways. We immediately set out to expand the "store" to include living quarters for my mother, father, sister, and me. I don't remember the actual move, but the first thing I do remember is the pain shooting through my left thumb as my thumbnail peeled back into the quick. Suddenly I realized that I was trying to trim my fingernails with my grandfather's pocket knife! (I'm sure I had seen "the men" do it that way.) At that point, as we were standing in the back yard, and I was screaming in pain, I realized that I had no memory prior to that startling and rude "awakening." I vaguely remember looking to my right and seeing piles of lumber and other building materials (destined to become the walls, ceiling, and roof of our new home).

So that day, way before the advent of video recorders, and several years before we got our first TV, my mind's camcorder started the genesis of this book that I am sharing with you now. Although Mules In The Fast Lane covers a lot of history, it is not a historical document. Neither is it merely an autobiographical journal or diary of my life. It is, rather, a collection of memorable events, hopefully laden with "life lessons" and moral principles that will help others experience them and enrich their lives as well. I elected to leave out most of the "bad stuff" (in retrospect, there really wasn't that much of that). In doing this, I hope to leave the reader feeling better about his or her own life, because one can choose to be negative or positive; I simply chose to be positive.

Many people may read this book and be inclined to say, "That's not the way it happened" or "That's not the way it was." And they will probably be right. The stories are written exactly as I remember them, and are true to the best of my recollection. When names are used, the first names are usually the same, but most last names have been changed to protect their privacy and anonymity. The stories are not necessarily in chronological order, but are arranged in series so that they "roll with the flow" of my childhood. Some are funny, some are sad, but all are poignant and full of roller coaster ups and downs that made me who I am today.

INTRODUCTION

I grew up just outside of the little southern town of Luverne in rural Crenshaw County, Alabama, about 50 miles from the Florida state line. As my cognitive functioning started to kick in, it didn't take long for me to realize that, economically speaking, we were not at the top of the heap. I will always remember an old colored man—his name was "Berry"—who used to, every so often, ride his mule and Sears and Roebuck wagon (really!) to the little Mom and Pop grocery store we owned. Periodically, he and his mule would get run off—or bumped off—the highway by some hurried motorist who just couldn't wait for them to move on. I remember thinking, "Well, at least we're better off than ol' Berry; at least we have a car!"

Now, don't get me wrong; we weren't poverty stricken, and we never "went hungry," but suffice it to say, there were quite a few townspeople who had a lot more than we did. But we were rich in other ways. Our family was a very close-knit one, and early on, both my paternal and maternal grandparents were still living, along with a "passel" of aunts, uncles, and cousins on both sides of the family. Therefore, I thought it prudent at this point to identify some of the "main characters" so that their names will be recognizable as their stories unfold later.

First and foremost, there was my mother, to whom I owe most of my "good" traits. She was loved by all, and although I called her Mother, she was also known as Lillie, Miss Lillie, Aunt Lillie, Mama, and Granny. Then there was my father, to whom I owe my respect for (and fear of!) the business side of life. He taught me to pay my bills, and also that the customer is always right. As with most southern fathers, I called him Daddy, but he was also known as Dad, John, Johnny, John William, Uncle John, Uncle Johnny, and Big Daddy. My sister, Jean, was two years older than me, but only one year ahead of me in school. Because of a school board ruling, she was almost seven years old when she started. That ruling was changed the following year, and I was allowed to start when I was still five. One had to be six years old by the 15th of January, and my birthday was January 6th.

My paternal grandmother was affectionately known by almost everyone as Annie, and was even called that by my father. My paternal grandfather's name was Mitchell Monroe Moody, and was known by his grandchildren as Daddy Moody. He had a brother named Isaiah Prim Moody, but everyone called him simply, Buddy. They had a sister named Nina, whom Buddy always called "Shug." Daddy Moody, Annie, Buddy, and Nina all lived in the same house.

My father's brother was Vernon, and was ten years younger than my father. (Another brother was born between them, but died at birth.) He was sometimes called Uncle Vernon. Vernon married Faye (sometimes called Aunt Faye), who already had a daughter named Nancy. Nancy became an immediate member of the family, and has been considered, over the years, as much of a blood relative as Vernon and Faye's other three children, Terry, Larry, and Cynthia, who were born later. Aubrey Spivey was my grandmother, Annie's nephew, and lived with my grandparents for several years, and worked on the farm.

On my mother's side was my maternal grandmother, Myrtle, also known as Mama Norman. My maternal grandfather's name was Brock, who was also known as Daddy Norman. My mother had a brother named Carl, but was known by everyone as "Doc." Doc lived with my grandparents until he married Dycia, who also became a "blood" relative and gave birth to my two beloved cousins, Glenna and Raymond. My mother had a younger brother, also named Raymond, who was killed in World War II. Although I never knew him, his memory dominated my mother's family for many years after his death.

Also on my mother's side were several aunts and uncles, like Uncle Coy and Aunt Ruby, Uncle Willie and Aunt Rebie, Uncle Onist and Aunt Kate, all of whom were as colorful as their names.

Honorable mention would be my father's eight first cousins,

whom my grandparents took in after their father (Daddy Moody's brother, Marcus) died and their mother, Emma, was unable to care for them. Their names were Sarah, Norene, Alice, Dorothy, Barbara, Gerald, Dalton, and Marcus Jr. Some of my cousins mentioned later are children of these eight first cousins of my father.

CHAPTER ONE

Life Kicks Into Second Gear

There's a lot of fuzziness between my first memory in the back yard at The Triangle and my sister starting the first grade. I guess there wasn't much of significance to hold on to at that time. But there's nothing like a pretty little blond-haired, blue-eyed girl with pigtails to jog a boy's memory.

And that is exactly what happened when Jean came home one day with her school pictures, along with some she had traded with friends. One of those was a picture of Nonie, a tall (even for first grade) beautiful girl who was to become Jean's lifelong best friend. Nonie's mother had passed away, and later our mother sort of "adopted" her. She was the youngest of six children, and her father was a rough, tough, gruff-talking, but very successful farmer who owned his own cotton gin. Usually, if you heard the "si-reen" during cotton picking season, you'd know it was probably Mr. Irvin's cotton gin that had gotten plugged up and caught on fire. Nonie spent countless hours at The Triangle after school, because it was easier for her to stop off at our house and "play" than to make the longer trip out to her house. And if she went home, she'd just have to fend for herself, since farming didn't leave much time for babysitting by her father. After she and Jean started the first grade, Jean told me how they learned to plait Nonie's hair into pigtails by practicing on pine needles taken from the school yard. It seemed that God must have made them that way because they had exactly three needles in a cluster, making it ideal for braiding. They used to bring boxes full home for me to "practice" on too.

You'd have to say that Nonie was my first love, and since she and

Jean were often inseparable, I was constantly tagging along as they played with their dolls or built "toad frog houses" out in the yard. Making toad frog houses was a favorite pastime of kids in those days. They were made by packing mounds of dirt around our bare feet, then carefully pulling our feet out, creating the "house" we pretended to occupy with "toad frogs," toy cars, or imaginary characters we conjured up in our minds. My love for Nonie was never to be consummated, however, as she always considered me more of a brother than a "boyfriend." Even today, when I see her, I joke that as soon as her husband dies, I'm going to marry her!

Those times when I wasn't chasing Nonie around, I was spending time with other little friends who would pop up in the neighborhood from time to time. Out in the open field directly behind The Triangle was a tiny two-room house where Jimmy and Mary Ann lived with their parents, Bud and Cumi. Jimmy and Mary Ann were the first friends Jean and I had, as they were already living there when we moved to The Triangle. Jimmy was slightly older than Jean, and Mary Ann was just a little younger than me, so we immediately became fast, lifelong friends. Bud was a slightly built man with a perpetual smile and a gentle, mild manner. His wife, Cumi was a stoically assertive, hard-working woman who loved her husband and children with an endearing passion.

During those "growing up years," I have many fond memories of hours spent at their house. My funniest memory of Cumi was after they moved away to northern Crenshaw County to a little community called Highland Home. Cumi developed some sort of gastrointestinal malady which caused her to belch uncontrollably. This condition persisted for some time, and the four of us would be playing happily at their house when Cumi would begin burping and trumpeting with reckless abandon, sending us children into fits of roaring laughter. It would be hard to say, during those episodes, who was making the most noise!

In those days, everyone had to be extremely frugal, and I didn't realize how spoiled I had become living in a grocery store. Anytime any of my little friends would come over, I was always generous in "sharing the bounty." In fact, I achieved quite a reputation for my hearty appetite and constant pilfering of food from the store. One neighbor/customer in particular named Julius tormented me unmercifully about it. His standard greeting to me for years (even years after it should have ceased) was, "Go to eatin', boy!" Anytime I saw old Julius coming, I'd grab a snack and unwrap it, knowing he was going to accuse me anyway.

The reality of how good we had it, food-wise, was brought home to me one day when I was visiting Jimmy in Highland Home. After a long day of playing and calorie burning, I suddenly realized I was starving, and asked Jimmy what they had to eat. Being used to choosing whatever I wanted—and as much as I wanted—to eat, I was sure Jimmy had a similar arrangement at his house. Wrong! Shortly, we found ourselves peering into their nearly bare refrigerator looking for something, *anything*, to make a sandwich out of. To my dismay, Jimmy pulled out a jar with a single slice of pineapple in it! "We can make a sandwich out of this," he announced. Now I wasn't a mathematical whiz, but this picture didn't add up for me. There were two of us and only one pineapple slice. It didn't take a rocket scientist to figure that somebody was going to get left out. I kind of hoped that Jimmy—seeing as how I was his guest—would let me have it. Not! However, since he didn't want to appear too selfish, he pulled a sharp knife out of the silverware drawer, and with the precision of a master diamond cutter, split that pineapple ring into two paper thin slices from which we made two meager sandwiches. I couldn't wait to get back to The Triangle, and never again took the bountiful supply of food we had in the store for granted.

LIFE LESSON NUMBER ONE

Appreciate first loves, good friends, and food; you never know how long you'll have them.

CHAPTER TWO

School Days (It Smells Like Bananas!)

There was a time when school teaching was considered the noblest of professions. The children in a teacher's classroom were like her own (there were few, if any, male elementary teachers at that time), and she taught and exhorted them exactly as if they were "family," even leading them in daily prayer and Bible reading. A survey of my teachers from first through sixth grades (called grammar school) revealed only two who had ever been married, and only one of those who had children of her own. All the more reason for those dedicated souls, each year, to "adopt" a new family of kids. We didn't have public kindergarten back then, so most of us started our school careers right into the first grade—sink or swim.

All that said, I felt anything but a family atmosphere on my first day of school. My mother had provided the majority of my care from birth to school age (except for her short stint at the local "sewing factory"), so she was the center and totality of my world. I'm sure she must have talked to me about my going to school some day, but I took none of this seriously until that awful, gray September morning in 1949 when Mother deposited me in the middle of Hell and walked away with me screaming my lungs out. (The only thing familiar that fateful morning was the smell of bananas. I later learned that these were favorite lunch box "stuffers" for kids who brought their lunches.)

My sister, Jean, was starting second grade, and came to be my salvation that first year. I don't remember consciously "plotting" to

7

get home, but I found that, if I soiled my pants daily, I could get a lot of attention and possibly even make it home. When that didn't work, I would simply go to sleep to pass the time. Many times I would awaken to find my room empty, and then creep down the hall to Jean's room where she would lovingly put her arm around me and wait for my teacher, Miss Irene, to come and haul me back to my room. This scenario was repeated dozens of times until I finally came to the realization that this was getting me nowhere fast (except maybe a trip back through the first grade), and it was only by the grace of God that I passed to the second grade.

The school caught fire and burned to the ground a few weeks after I started, and I always wondered if anyone thought I had set it.

LIFE LESSON NUMBER TWO

Like it or not, learning starts early; accept this, and it'll save you a lot of crap later.

CHAPTER THREE

My First Lesson In Decision Making

After the initial shock and trauma of starting school, I finally settled down to some real "book learnin'." But most of the good stuff I learned in that first year didn't come from books. For starters, I learned I couldn't depend on Mother Nature to hold off my bowel movements until I got home so my mother could "wipe me." I also learned that, if you hang upside down from the monkey bars and drop off onto your head, you'll break your collarbone. And right after that happens, and you cry and scream bloody murder that you want to go home, you won't get to go unless you give the teacher a darn good reason. (I didn't want to tell her I was stupid enough to drop off onto my head; I just knew I heard something crack when I landed, and it hurt like Hell.)

And finally I learned that when a teacher tries to talk and reason and explain, and that doesn't work for her, she kicks into corporal punishment mode and whips out the paddle. Hence, my first spanking at the tender age of five by someone other than my mother. Our first grade teacher, Miss Irene Morris, was loved by all. She was a gentle, sweet-spirited spinster who genuinely loved her children, and no one—especially a "Mama's Boy" like me—would have ever thought she would resort to such "cruel" measures to teach us discipline. As was the custom in first grade, afternoon naps were a mandatory part of the curriculum, and everyone was expected to comply—ADHD or not! As noted previously, I had had plenty of experience in the nap department. And when awake, I wasn't particularly hyperactive

(Ritalin didn't come along until years later), but I did sometimes have a problem making up my mind and sticking to it.

Well, all this wishy-washiness was about to change when Miss Irene gave us the choice, at nap time, of laying our head on our arm at our desk, or lying on our towel on the floor. She stressed, before leaving the room, that once our decision was made, we couldn't change our mind. I don't remember which decision I made, but I do remember I couldn't turn my brain off in order to get to sleep. (In fact, I still have an insomnia problem to this day.) I think this was also the day I learned the principle—if not the adage—that "An idle mind is the devil's workshop." My reasoning went something like this: *Do I really have to stay here? There are a lot of people in here; if I move, she won't remember where I was. I'm uncomfortable. I'm not sleepy. I need to move. Here I go!*"

Well, I still wasn't asleep when Miss Irene re-entered the room, radar scanning, and immediately lifted me up and escorted me to the paddling corner. Of course, the actual paddling didn't hurt as much as the humiliation of it all. Suffice it to say, I became disciplined that day and learned a valuable lesson in decision-making.

I had only one other encounter—or near encounter—with "the paddle." It happened later in elementary school during the football season. In today's modern electronic age, it's hard to believe the primitive way we charged admission to our local football games. The "ticket booth" looked as though it had been brought over on the Mayflower. It was about four foot square (only one person could fit in there, and he couldn't be fat), and it was covered on top and three and a half sides with rusty tin. The floor was obviously dirt, which grew up in weeds in the off season. To say it was "dilapidated" would have been a severe understatement. Many of the nails that held the tin sides in place had come loose, allowing the panels to flap noisily in the slightest breeze. This proved to be great entertainment for several of us boys, and on dull, quiet, windless days, we would find any number of different items—rocks, sticks, tree limbs, and feet—to beat on those loose panels, just to make noise and liven things up!

Well, this didn't set too well with one of the football coaches. His name was Coach Norton. I always thought his name sounded like "Snortin'," and you just didn't want to get on his bad side. He must have been in a particularly foul mood that day (maybe he'd lost too many games). After an especially fun episode of tin-banging and noise-making that obviously agitated the man, about ten of us found ourselves at "Snortin' Norton's" mercy. He lined us up and ordered us to bend over. Then came the question, "How many licks do y'all think y'all oughta have?" He strode by each of us in drill sergeant fashion, slapping his three-foot paddle into the palm of his hand with each step. Silence. We weren't sure if he really wanted us to answer the question, or if he just wanted us to suffer while we thought about it.

This might have been one of my first attempts at manipulation (or diplomacy), because I remember thinking—since nobody else was saying anything—that maybe if I said, "Oh, about 10..." then perhaps Snortin' Norton would see I'm not trying to get out of anything, and he'd have mercy on me and let me go! Still, something kept me from saying a word (probably a good idea), and after what seemed like an entire school year, we were turned loose, never to abuse ticket booths again.

I never see a ticket-taker or a ticket booth to *any* event without thinking about the lesson I learned that day: There's a time to make noise and a time to keep your mouth shut!

LIFE LESSON NUMBER THREE

Most decisions are easy to make; it's sometimes the consequences that are hard!

CHAPTER FOUR

Daniel Teaches Me "The Bird"

Over the years, I learned many "things" in elementary (grammar) school, high school, and college—and not all of these from certified teachers. One of my earliest "lessons" was from a little boy named Daniel, when he and I were in the second grade. For some reason, Daniel and I "hit it off" as friends, and I can't tell you why. I don't remember his last name, nor do I remember anything outstanding about him, other than his appearance and the lesson he taught me. He wasn't really fat, but he wasn't really skinny either, and he had a head full of unkempt sandy hair that always looked like it had been cut with a dull knife. His face looked as though he had already started shaving (was it dirty, or was it just "rough?"). His clothes were, at best, "adequate," and perhaps the affinity between us was that we both knew we didn't quite "measure up" in the fashion department.

The second grade was a major transitional period. You were no longer the beginner you were in first grade. For example, you were no longer *printing* your words; now you were *writing* them, just like a grown up. I recall that I had pretended to write in cursive before I started to school and would ask Mother, "What am I writing?" Of course, she would always make up something, and I remember thinking how smart I was. Now that I was learning to do the real thing, I decided to show off for Daniel, and wrote my first full word in cursive, "tit," which he and I got a huge chuckle out of. Somehow we must have known that word was a no-no, because we didn't show it to the teacher, and I erased it as soon as we finished laughing about it.

Then, one day, there must have been a lull on the education freeway (maybe it was recess or play period, or the teacher was preoccupied), because Daniel and I were engaged in mindless chatter, and he asked, "Can you do this?" With his right hand raised high, he showed me the most perfect "bird!" Now, I don't know if he knew that this was also a no-no, but if he did, he didn't tell *me*. I was always excited about learning new "things" (after all, I was in the second grade, and had just learned to write the word "tit!"), so of course, I said, "No, show me how!" And thus began my most memorable lesson of the second grade. "Well, you take this finger here, and bend it back like this." (He was helping me with mine.) "No, keep this one straight; then you bend this one back like this; now *you* try it."

I'll have you know, I must have been a natural, because by the end of the day, I had mastered the move so well, I was able to perform it with flawless perfection for my mother that night. You can imagine the scene as I proudly announced to her, "Hey Mother, look what I learned at school today," and proceeded to show her how to do it too! I'm not sure if Mother knew what it meant or not, but she was gracious about it, and replied, "Oh, that's nice…." It wasn't until years later I realized the true "meaning" of that most invaluable "lesson" I learned from little Daniel, and of course, have found countless applications for it since.

LIFE LESSON NUMBER FOUR

It's not the lesson you learn that's important; it's how well you use it later that counts.

CHAPTER FIVE

Annette And The Slide

Nowadays we take so much for granted. Sometimes we don't stop to think "how things used to be," and how blessed we are today. My sister and I are baby boomers, which meant our parents were products of The Depression. I remember Mother telling us once how thrilled she was one particularly "fruitful" Christmas when she got an orange in her stocking! She felt very fortunate, she said, because many of her friends got nothing at all. Relatively speaking, compared to today, we felt equally deprived. In the small town near where we grew up, there were very few "playground amenities," except maybe an old tire hanging from a tree for a swing, or a creek to wade in.

After I recovered from the shock of getting out from under my mother's protective wing at home, I discovered that being at school actually had its own unique set of "perks." For example, it had a full playground with swings, monkey bars, and see-saws. By the time I made it to the third grade, the school had acquired some pretty neat equipment. Everybody's favorite was the slide, which mysteriously appeared one Monday morning on the playground. Some of us "country kids" had never seen one, and it caused quite a stir. At every recess and play period, it would cause a near riot, and after its sudden arrival, the swings and monkey bars weren't nearly as popular. If you could manage to get to the line, which invariably formed quickly, you might be fortunate enough to slide down it twice before the bell rang summoning us back to class. I don't remember any actual fights, but there was plenty of competition as all six grades jockeyed for a favorable position in the slide's coveted line.

Some of the kids discovered that, if you put some pine straw under your butt, you could slide down faster. I upped the ante one day, and achieved even more speed when I brought a piece of waxed paper and sat on it before taking the plunge. What a ride! The other kids envied me because I always remembered to tuck a folded piece in my pocket for a fast getaway down the slope!

It wasn't long after the new slide arrived that I had an unforgettable "accident" on it. As usual, the line stretched for "miles," and I was certain the bell would ring before I could even get down the first time. So, with waxed paper in hand, I was preceded by Annette Sims, a rambunctious first grader, who I knew wouldn't waste any time flying down ahead of me. We inched up the ladder which had bars on either side that made loops at the top for holding on as the slider positioned his or her rear end on the top of the six-foot incline. I had made it almost to the crest, and was happily surveying the world and anticipating the thrill to come, when disaster struck. Preoccupied with the view, I didn't realize I had ventured a mite too close to little Annette's back end. The bells I heard ringing came not from the school, but from inside my head, as both of her heels pummeled my chin in her haste to swing her legs over the apex and make her descent.

Stars came out, and birds started singing as I reeled from the impact. Still clutching my waxed paper accelerator, I managed to grab something metal with my free hand to keep from falling. Of course, no one (not even little Annette) knew I'd been hit, as they were all preoccupied with their own thrill-seeking. I don't remember making that trip down the slide that day, but I do remember the valuable lesson I learned: On your way to the top, don't crowd the person ahead of you. It just might be an ambitious female who's trying to get there too!

LIFE LESSON NUMBER FIVE

Be nice to people following you; they might get ahead of you someday!

CHAPTER SIX

Riding My Sister's Bicycle

As anyone who has older siblings knows, there is always that temptation by the parents to provide an unlimited supply of hand-me-downs for the younger ones. This can be a blessing, or it can be a curse. In my case, since my older sibling was a sister, it was the latter. I was what people often referred to as a "Mama's Boy," and there was no denying it. But I was also very much a boy, with pocket knives, BB guns, skinned knees, and an endless variety of pets. I liked being a Mama's Boy, as it definitely had its perks. For example, I never had to fight my own fights, especially with my sister, Jean. All I had to do was scream like I was being murdered, and from the corner of the ring would spring my mother, swinging the paddle, switch, or some other weapon of defense against the evil one. Sometimes, though, Mother tended to be a little too over-protective, and would butt in to protect me even when I didn't need or want it. I remember one day, after a particularly "mother-hen-clucking session," retreating into a nearby closet, turning the light off, savoring the privacy, and thinking how great it was to have my own "space."

Then I discovered my sister's bicycle. After making short work of the learning process, and enduring the inevitable skinned knees and wounded pride, I found the road to freedom and independence on that two-wheeled marvel. For the first time in my life, I could "drive away" by myself and go to places I'd never been, like the far corner of the pasture next to The Triangle, or that little fishing hole down the road I didn't even know was there. My mother's strict rule, though, was that I stay off the highway, and ride only on the side of the road, or take the "back way" on some unbeaten path less traveled.

I'm not sure when it hit me, but somewhere in time there came the realization that boys' and girls' bicycles were different. I believe it was shortly after one of my friends saw me riding Jean's bike and fell over laughing at the sight of a Mama's Boy riding his sister's bicycle. That's when my quest for my own (boy's) bicycle began. In addition to the fact that my use of Jean's bike was constantly interfering with her desire to take her own occasional trip on it, I found myself unmercifully harangued by friends who would see me daily violating the boy rule of never riding a girl's bicycle. For years, I endured the "abuse" of seeing my sister get a new bicycle while I was handed down her old one.

So, one day I decided it was time to take matters into my own hands. Now, I had studied this bicycle thing for years, and it seemed to me that the only difference between a boy's bicycle and a girl's bicycle was that little bar thing that extended between the seat and the handle bars. It was missing on a girl's bicycle. It appeared to me that, if I could put that little bar thing on one of Jean's hand-me-downs—presto—I would have my own *boy's* bicycle! Having lived through The Depression, Mother and Daddy—like most people their age—rarely threw anything away. They never knew when times would get hard and they might need it (whatever *it* was). This is sometimes referred to as "hoarding," but my parents just saw it as being thrifty.

This practice of theirs was fortunate for me because, in Daddy's stash, I found a perfect piece of old galvanized pipe that looked like it could be used to make that little bar thing. My challenge now was to get somebody to cut it the right length, drill a couple of holes to secure it to the frame, and I'd have a genuine boy's bicycle. This was really a big deal for me, and I figured that, if I could get it to work, it would save me from my obvious destiny of growing up to be a "girly man." I even found some spray paint that almost matched the bike after "installing" the bar, and the metamorphosis was complete! I still remember bursting with pride the first time I mounted my "new" bicycle and sped off with eager anticipation to my favorite fishing hole.

The epilogue to this story is that, even though I now had my own *boy's* bicycle, I knew it wasn't the real thing, so I proceeded to put the final phase of my plan into action. I'm not sure how long I rolled the scheme around in my head, but I do remember that part of my plan was to hammer away at my parents until they finally gave in.

I wasn't much of a salesman, but I had learned how to "manipulate" to get my needs met. I knew I had to spring the trap on a Saturday morning when Daddy was around, as he usually worked his insurance route on Saturday afternoon, and of course, the stores would be closed on Sunday. In the final scene, we are sitting at the kitchen table eating lunch. This was after several days of my moping and dropping hints about bicycles, and my parents continually reminding me that new bicycles cost a lot of money (about $60 at the time and probably well over Daddy's weekly salary). I was picking at my food (as planned), and the silence was deafening, broken only by the sound of forks clinking plates.

Mother finally broke the silence. "Mike, why aren't you eating? Aren't you hungry?"

Of course, everyone knew I was still brooding over this bicycle thing. So, now was my chance. I was going for the jugular. With conjured tears and a quake in my voice that could have won me an Academy Award, I closed the deal.

"W-well, you know, I'm not going to be a little boy forever…"

In less than ten seconds, Daddy and I were out the door, on our way to Mr. Al Tarver's store, where most of the new bicycles (including my sister's) came from! The financial arrangements were made in the "showroom," and then the announcement came.

"O.K., Mike, go around back and get your bicycle."

I raced, heart pounding, half stumbling, half flying, outside to the stockroom where the shiny new two-toned green Schwinn awaited its master.

But, Good Lord, the thing was so big, I had to look up to see the seat—and that glorious bar across it! Plus, it had a horn, a headlight, and white sidewall balloon tires! I mounted it in one flying leap, and sped around the corner toward my beaming father. The excitement of the moment was diminished only by the pain in my groin as the revered bar found its mark squarely between my legs in my first attempt at disembarking the giant vehicle.

I recovered quickly, but not only did I learn a good lesson in *boy's* bicycle riding, it was also the first time I fully realized the distinct advantage of riding my sister's bicycle!

LIFE LESSON NUMBER SIX

Don't look a gift horse in the mouth; it might bite you in the end.

CHAPTER SEVEN

The Bravest Kid In School

Most of us knew kids in school that we looked up to. The boy who ran the winning touchdown the last few seconds of the game; the champion of the spelling bee; the one who had a special talent for art. Boys, particularly, were impressed with other boys who showed exceptional courage in the face of adversity. A couple of my classmates were injured, and I remember thinking how brave they were, having had to go through the trauma. For example, a friend named Pat ran into some barbed wire, which cut him up pretty badly. Another friend, Stanley, ran through a plate glass door and almost bled to death. Both were real "heroes" for a while after those accidents.

However, there was a particularly poignant incident that happened one day at school in "Assembly" that gave me a whole new perspective on bravery. Assemblies were gatherings in the school auditorium when all the grades came together for announcements, skits, and other important functions. During this particular assembly program, one of the upper classes had some activities and "talents" their teachers wanted to share with the school. One of those was a song entitled The Wayward Wind—a popular song of the day—which was to be performed by a sweet, but rather shy girl named Julia Faye.

Our principal, Mr. Harlan, was a stern-faced, no-nonsense, take-no-prisoners kind of guy who demanded utter peace and quiet during these programs. His voice sounded like an amplified public address system, and needless to say, he never used a microphone. He would quietly and deliberately walk out on the stage, and peer out over the throng through small rimless glasses. He would always give the congregation a few seconds to discover his presence, and then raise

31

his right hand, curling the ring and little fingers down to meet his thumb, leaving his index and middle fingers raised in a final warning to be silent. Within 15 seconds, you could hear a pin drop. You did not want to be the last one making noise when Mr. Harlan walked out on that stage.

After a few meaningless announcements by Mr. Harlan and one or two presentations by other students, it was time for sweet Julia Faye to perform. I didn't really know Julia Faye, but I knew who she was, as it was a fairly small school, and "everybody knew everybody." I don't think anyone had ever heard Julia Faye sing, so we were all wondering if she could pull it off. After positioning herself in the center of the stage, she choked out the first verse—without accompaniment—then promptly forgot the words!

Anyone who has ever had to "perform" before a live audience knows about stage fright and butterflies. But to forget the words in the middle of a song—without accompaniment—is the ultimate nightmare. Julia Faye stood there for several seconds, wide-eyed and trembling. The crowd grew restless, and at first, began to nervously titter, then exploded in uproarious laughter, sending poor Julia Faye running for cover. It seemed unfair the way people were laughing at this unfortunate soul, and at this point, most of us were thinking that Julia Faye's singing career was probably over.

But then, something short of a miracle occurred. Julia Faye slowly walked back out on stage! As the crowd settled into stunned silence, brave shy Julia Faye raised her head, fixed her eyes in a determined glare, and with the courage no one in the audience could believe, belted out the entire song flawlessly! Even the cruelest skeptics in the crowd were impressed, and the thunderous applause was deafening.

I never spoke to Julia Faye, but I'm sure she went down in history that day as one of the bravest kids to ever participate in "Assembly."

LIFE LESSON NUMBER SEVEN

Do what you have to do; courage and bravery come when you least expect them.

CHAPTER EIGHT

Other "Life Lessons" Learned In School

By adulthood, most of us have learned that life is not fair. My major beef with schools today is that they teach facts and figures, but rarely do they teach "life lessons." In our zeal to keep church and state separate, we've taken many of our time-honored traditions such as prayer and Bible reading out of public schools, lest we be labeled fanatics trying to cram religious doctrine down hapless children's throats. Whether a lot of the good life lessons I learned in school back then were a result of religious influences, I can't say with certainty. However, I won't discount that influence either.

Originally the title for this book was to be <u>You Had To Play Football</u>. It came from the notion I had as a child that there were certain boys who were the most popular because they were, first and foremost, star athletes. And, of course, football was *the* sport to star in.

But, as I progressed with the book, other "lessons" started coming out in the stories. The work then became more than just an account of my disappointments and failures as an athlete. One of those memories stuck with me, however, and begged to be included.

Although I was a boy to the core, and very active when "at play," I was not what you would call athletic. Many of my friends had fathers who spent time with them and encouraged them to participate in sports, the most prominent of which were football, baseball, and basketball. I didn't really care that my father didn't push me in that direction, because, frankly, I wasn't interested anyway. In retrospect, not all the boys in my school were star athletes, and I certainly wasn't the only one who wasn't. But every now and then, it would be made very clear how important athletic prowess was when my peers would decide to play ball, and we'd have to "choose up sides." Whenever they shifted into ball-playing mode, I would usually high-tail it somewhere else, not wanting to embarrass my friends who would be forced to pick me as their very last choice to be on their team.

One day on the playground I hung around a little too long, and some of the guys decided to play a game called "21 butt beat." I'd never heard of the game, but the object was simple. A bunch of boys lined up to shoot basketball hoops, and each successful dunk was good for a score of "1." As each player reached the final score of 21, he would drop out and cheer the others on. Although this was not a "team" game, and we didn't have to choose up sides, this one was worse because, with 21 butt beat, there was no winning team, but only one single loser—the last one to score 21 points. And even worse, the loser had to keep trying until he sank his 21 baskets. Then the final and ultimate humiliation was that, when the loser scored his last point, he was "rewarded" by being forced to hold onto the post while the rest of the boys lined up and "beat his butt" with the basketball.

That was probably the longest basketball "game" in history for me, and I still remember the pain, not in my butt, but in my face, as I forced myself to laugh while crying inside from the humiliation. The lesson I learned from that experience, eventually, was that we all have our own individual talents we have to develop.

I later became quite well known for my acting abilities and was featured in several "major productions" at the school. The "roar of the grease paint and the smell of the crowd" more than compensated for my feelings of failure as an athlete, and I later spent 20 years in the broadcasting field as a result of the desire to express my talents in a less strenuous way than "busting my butt" on the basketball court.

Teachers in those days had their own unique problems to deal with too. In fact, it is difficult to believe some of the things that were required of our teachers. Having successfully completed the third grade with one of my favorite teachers, Miss Grace Head, I was looking forward to moving on to the fourth grade. I was delighted to find out that she was going to be my teacher again. But what was incredible about it was that she was also going to be teaching the third grade again—at the same time! When I hear people complaining today about overcrowded classrooms, I think back to that year with the third grade at the front of the classroom, and us fourth graders in the rear of the classroom. If Miss Grace ever complained about having to teach two classes in one room, she never did it openly.

One of the highlights of the fourth grade was when I learned to recite the 67 counties of Alabama. My father had always been a straight "A" student (in the same school my sister and I later attended), and he didn't require anything of us that he couldn't do himself. I came to appreciate his learning (and teaching) methods, and found them nothing short of ingenious at the time. I learned not to ask Daddy for help too often, because he had an "impatient" streak that permitted him to allow his students only one or two failures. After that, you were on your own! Regarding the 67 counties, he figured if a person could memorize the alphabet with only 26 letters, it should be a piece of cake to memorize the 67 counties by doing it just 12 at a time. So that's how I did it. I would memorize 12 counties each night, then "string 'em together," as he put it. Miss Grace had given us several days to learn them, and I still remember the feeling of elation when she asked (early), "Can anybody recite the counties yet?" and I raised my hand.

To this day, I can still recite those 67 counties faster than anyone can count them. The lesson learned? "Yard by yard, life is hard; inch by inch (or in this case 12 by 12), it's a cinch!"

The following year, in "Miss Madie's" fifth grade, I learned another valuable life lesson. I always knew there were some kids who were "smarter" than me. No matter how hard I tried, there were always those two or three kids who consistently scored higher than me on tests, homework assignments, etc. My good friend, Joe, was not one of those kids. That's why this life lesson was so hard to swallow.

I was a pretty good student most of the time, and almost always did my homework. The key words are "almost always." For some reason, one day I had not completed my homework. I had rationalized that Miss Madie wouldn't ask for it. She rarely did, and I figured I could always "finish it later." It wasn't that I was a procrastinator; I just sometimes worked better under pressure. Well, wouldn't you know, on this particular day, Miss Madie uttered the dreaded words, "O.K., pass your homework up." I guess she saw me "fumbling around," because she zeroed in on me and asked, "Mike, did you do your homework?" Timidly, I replied, "Well, I didn't quite finish it." I still don't know why she had singled me out. Maybe she wanted to make an example out of me to drive home the importance of doing homework; I don't know. I just know that, at that point, she lost it. "O.K., everybody who did their homework, get over here!" she barked. "The rest of you get over there," she pointed.

Now, I knew that Joe had not done *any* of his homework, but incredibly, he stood up and walked over to the side of the room where all the "done homework" kids were gathering! I thought, well, if he can get away with it, so can I. After all, I had done *most* of my homework. So I headed over there too. But ol' Eagle Eyes Madie wasn't through with me yet. She stopped me in my tracks, and commanded, "Nooo, Mike, you get over there with the *do-nothin' crowd!*" and literally escorted me to the other side of the room. Embarrassment took on a whole new meaning, and I caught Joe's eye as I passed by, and the sound of snickering from the "smarties" pierced my ears.

This was probably the first time I realized that life was not fair. At that moment, I felt violated! I wanted justice! I wanted to blurt out how Joe hadn't done *his* homework, and wasn't being herded over to the *"do-nothin' crowd."* I wanted at least *some* credit for doing *most* of my homework. But none of this mattered to Miss Madie. There was to be no justice today.

Not only did I learn that day that life was not fair. I also learned that sometimes it's better to just let things go. I've often thought what would have happened to my friendship with Joe if I had "ratted" on him. Joe knew he was wrong. And, deep down, I think I knew Miss Madie was right. I indeed hadn't done my homework, and it had nothing to do with whether or not Joe—or anybody else—had done theirs. You don't *almost* make a touchdown. You either do the right thing or you don't. Joe never mentioned the incident again, and neither did I. We remained friends throughout the remainder of our school years. And I never failed to do my homework after that day.

Another incident that seemed unfair also occurred in the fifth grade. For years our regimen had been the same at school. Spend a couple of hours in class, take recess, have more class time, go to lunch, more class, play period, class, then go home. By the fifth grade, most of us who had been at our little school since Day One were pros in the drill. That's why it was such a shocker the day one of the second grade teachers, Miss Ailene, went crazy and suddenly "changed the rules." Miss Ailene was a rather pleasant-looking sophisticated middle-aged woman with thick, lightly-tinted glasses and perfectly styled gray hair. It was common knowledge that she was "well-to-do" and probably didn't have to work. She had not been my teacher in second grade, but I knew who she was.

As usual, that morning, we were all enjoying recess when Mother Nature called me. As I had done for years (at least since half way through the first grade!), I headed inside for the little boys' room. I had taken about five steps inside the back door when Miss Ailene broke my stride.

"Where are you going?" she demanded.

Somewhat taken aback that she was even questioning me about something I had done since I was a freshman, I replied, "I'm going to the bathroom." I'm certain that I did not, in any way, appear disrespectful in voice or manner.

Suddenly, Miss Ailene erupted, "You can't just come in and go to the bathroom!" And with that, she grabbed me by the arm, and slapped me repeatedly six or eight times on the side of my face.

As soon as it started, it was over, and Miss Ailene turned me loose. Stunned, I staggered back outside, still trying to make sense of what had just happened. About a year earlier, I had recovered from the measles, which, I was told, had "settled" in my left ear, causing total deafness in that ear. Unfortunately, Miss Ailene had no knowledge of this, and had pounded my "good ear," endangering the hearing in that ear as well.

By the end of recess, I was still obviously shaken and upset, and, when questioned by my own teacher, Miss Madie, simply told her the truth. (I knew better than to lie to Miss Madie!) My mother was called, and came to the school immediately. The rest of the day was sort of a blur, but I do remember that my mother handled the situation very well. Again, I don't know that "justice" was done that day, because I never heard of Miss Ailene being reprimanded or disciplined for her vicious act. Nor did she ever apologize to me or my mother. Over the years, I've tried to make excuses for her or come up with possible reasons for her doing what she did. Was she just having a bad day? Had I said or done something, unaware, that "set her off?" Had I just not heard about the "rules of recess" being changed only on that day? I could never fully explain it.

I had never made it a practice to read the obituary page, but for some reason, many years later, I inadvertently read about Miss Ailene's death in the newspaper. Although I had long since "forgiven" her, I've often wondered if that was God's way of giving me closure on the day Miss Ailene "boxed my ears."

LIFE LESSON NUMBER EIGHT

Life isn't fair, and it's better to forgive than receive. . .what you'll reap if you don't.

CHAPTER NINE

Learning From Failure

Henry Ford once said that we learn more from our failures than from our successes. It took me years to understand that, when a person fails a lot, it doesn't mean he or she is a *failure*. A failure is the person who has stopped trying. According to Henry Ford, a person who fails a lot should just be getting smarter.

Well, you couldn't tell my seventh grade history teacher (or my parents) that when I got my first test back. I made a 44, and it was my first failing grade of my school career. I had never liked history, and had never put much effort into trying to like it. It wasn't until I had lived through a good bit of it that I began to appreciate it!

Dejectedly, I brought the failing paper to show my parents, knowing that I would be able to offer no excuse for such a low grade. My sister was always very helpful (and usually a straight "A" student), but I hated to ask her for help. And when it came to really difficult issues (like history), Mother usually deferred to Daddy. Although he was a hard worker—in school and in his vocation—he liked to find easier ways to do—and learn—things. Working smarter, not harder was his philosophy. Other than helping me learn the 67 counties of Alabama, I remember his helping me with only one other thing related to school work: my multiplication table. Once he clued me in on his technique for learning the subject in question, he usually left me alone to do it myself. I liked that technique, and even today, I still prefer what work motivation theorists refer to as "Theory Y." In his book, The Human Side of Enterprise, Douglas McGregor holds that "people are basically creative, responsible, and intrinsically motivated to do good work to the extent that the work is challenging." And Daddy certainly made it challenging for me.

Regarding the failing history grade, the first question he asked me was not, as I had expected, "Why did you make such a low grade?" but rather, "Where do you sit in class?"

I explained that I sat in the back of the room next to the door so that, when the bell rang, I could get out of there.

"And do you take notes?" he asked.

"Well, I try," I answered feebly. I knew what Daddy was doing. He was thinking about my hearing impairment, and was wondering if I might be missing something by sitting in the back of the room.

"O.K., here's what I want you to do tomorrow," he said. "I want you to move up to the front row in class, as close to the teacher as you can get. Then I want you to look at your teacher. If you can take notes and look at your teacher at the same time, that's fine, but I want you to keep your eyes on that teacher."

And that was it. My father's lesson in dealing with failure: sit up front and keep your eyes on the teacher. Skeptical at first, I knew it was fruitless to argue with Daddy. I even decided to follow his advice in the rest of my classes as well, and from that day on, any time I was in class—and later attending workshops and seminars—I always sat up front and kept my eyes on the teacher. I made a "B" in history that year. Sometimes Father Does Know Best!

LIFE LESSON NUMBER NINE

When you find yourself at the bottom of the class, simply move up. . .to the front.

CHAPTER TEN

Moving Into The Attic

When my family moved to The Triangle, it was mostly an old store, and not really much of a home. Since I don't remember anything prior to that move, I had nothing to compare to what you would call a "normal" home.

But, my folks set about to make this run-down old store a home for us, and, eventually, there it was—with two bedrooms, a kitchen, a bathroom (plus a "public" restroom for customers), a living room (which came later), and a huge, dusty attic.

Since I wasn't able to bring any animals from the farm with me to The Triangle, I remember how excited I was one day when a Red Bird accidentally found its way through one of the cracks in the old structure and we chased that poor bird for a half hour before it finally escaped!

Some time after we finished the "home" part for living in, we painted the bedroom my sister, Jean, and I shared. Since she was older, she got to choose the color—pink. I didn't really care, because prior to that time, I'd only ever seen raw wood walls. What a treat to go to sleep surrounded by soothing pink walls and the smell of fresh paint! (Even now, my favorite color is pink.)

We later upgraded part of the south end of the store into a separate space we called the "living room," and covered it with some fancy green "cardboard" paneling. Compared to where we had come from, surely this was paradise!

It might seem a little strange today, but when my sister and I were growing up at The Triangle, not only did we share a bedroom, we also shared a bed. It didn't seem at all inappropriate at the time.

In fact, it made perfect sense, because there was plenty of room in a full-sized bed for two people, and it would just take up space and cost money to put another bed in that small room.

So, for years we became very "bonded," not only because of our close proximity, but because we were "family," and you just couldn't get any closer than that. "Enmeshment" later became a dirty word, but we didn't see this as a problem. I'm positive that those early years spent with my sister helped form my views and values about closeness in a family. The message was: "There's nothing more important than *family*."

All that said, as the years passed, I would find myself longing for some sense of privacy, especially as I approached my pre-adolescent years. I would not have friends over, because I didn't have a room of my own to "hang out" in and, as great as Jean was, sometimes a sister just got in the way!

My parents somehow must have sensed that both of us needed our own space, because they bought another bed and put it in the space we eventually called the living room. This room, then, became the "hub" of family activity and the place where everybody—including guests—congregated on any given day or night. Sometimes even customers would occasionally come in to "chat." So much for my own private space!

As a child, I was an avid reader, having devoured all of the Bobbsey Twins and Hardy Boys books in a short period of time. I also read magazines such as Popular Science and Popular Mechanics, and even "adult" magazines such as National Geographic, Life, and Look.

It was in one of those magazines that I found an article on turning attics into productive living space. I immediately cut the article out and showed it to my parents. I was further encouraged that we could do this by the fact that the family of a friend of mine named Pat had remodeled their attic with great results. They lived "in town," and I had seen it a couple of times. It was beautiful, as was their entire home. Jean and I thought they were rich because, well, they lived in town, and their house was made of brick! Their attic had been done in gorgeous "knotty-pine" paneling, exquisitely stained and varnished. It was perpetually new and fresh because of the smell and the sheen!

I'm not sure whether my insistence had anything to do with our eventual plans to "remodel." All I know is that we began to talk about it more and more. Every night when we would settle down to watch TV in my bedroom/our living room, I would pull that article out. I kept it folded up and neatly stuffed into the window frame behind the couch for easy retrieval and subsequent "selling" to my parents.

Not every night offered me the opportunity to pitch my idea, however, because, as long as the lights were on, The Triangle was open. This meant constant interruptions of *whatever* was going on in the living room, whether it was watching TV, doing homework, or just being together as a family. And let's not forget the nightly "turning of the antenna." Before the days of cable TV or satellites, there were antennae and—initially in our part of the country—only one UHF TV station fifty miles away. Depending on the weather, my father would make the nightly trek outside to twist the pole in an effort to get reception right. The ritual was the same every night.

"O.K. Daddy, that's it. Hold it right there! No, go back…stop… hold it…wait…no, you messed it up!"

His retort would also be the same. "How's *that*? What? Can you see it now…?"

And on it would go, until finally the reception was acceptable (but never good), or we resigned ourselves to watch the given program behind a flurry of electronic snow.

Eventually, after months (seemed like years) of "selling," begging, and cajoling, construction officially began on the "upstairs project." This was quite a learning experience. Until that time, I had never heard of—or seen, to my knowledge—sheetrock. What a great invention! You just tack it up, slap some putty on it, smooth it off and paint it, and presto! "Instant" colored walls!

With the installation of a dog house (aka, dormer) in each room, my sister and I had our own private window. On one end of the attic, we added a "den," and, on the other end, a huge walk-in bathroom, complete with a dresser made of two wooden apple crates and a nail keg for a stool. Mother expertly covered them with matching cloth for a very distinctive touch!

Although we were ecstatic about finally having our own bedrooms, Jean and I soon found that there were a couple of drawbacks to living in the attic. For one, summers were unbearable up there, and, during the day, it was literally uninhabitable. It would be so hot that, for years, she and I would scurry up to the attic for a few minutes, then rush downstairs and pretend for a few gloriously cool minutes that we had air-conditioning downstairs! The window fan stuck in the bathroom window cooled it down only at night, and then only late into the night or early morning as temperatures dropped outside.

Another problem was that space was of the essence, so a hallway was out of the question. Therefore, that privacy I had longed for "went out the window" every time my sister (or anyone else) had to go to the bathroom because they had to walk through my bedroom to get there.

But, nevertheless, it was a start, and a far cry from the days of one bed in the cramped little pink room we used to call *our* bedroom. Although not as private as I would've liked, the bedroom was *my own*, and I got to choose green for the color. (I had to choose a *different* color because, of course, Jean had chosen pink for her room.)

After we moved into the attic, I found out it wasn't a good idea to get Daddy riled up in the morning. Daddy had a way of waking my sister and me up on school days that was unmistakable and unforgettable. He was strictly business about it, and, all through high school, he took his "mission" very seriously. You never wanted to hear him say, "Don't make me come up there!"

His "official desk" in the corner of the kitchen was directly under my bedroom, and he was an early riser, sometimes getting up as early as 4:30 A.M. This gave him plenty of time to plan his day, part of which included getting Jean and me out of bed. I'd always been a "night owl," and for me, waking up was like pulling teeth every morning. Daddy had a broom stick he used to pound the ceiling above his desk. All the rooms downstairs were solid pine wood, including the ceilings, so when he started pounding, the sound would resonate throughout both floors, unmercifully jarring me out of my slumber. If he didn't hear footsteps above him within minutes, the pounding would resume with renewed fervor and volume. Needless to say, he never did have to "come up there."

That "attic" became *the* place for Jean and me and all our friends during our high school years. We each had our own AM radio (FM was virtually non-existent), and shared a stereo (something new at the time) in the den, which had replaced the original 45 RPM portable turntable that looked like a small suitcase when folded up. If we didn't have the best of everything, at least what we had was unique. Who else could boast their own private living quarters with the latest in entertainment technology, *plus* an unlimited supply of all the candy we cared to eat when our friends came to visit? We had been taught (finally!) to be responsible when "taking from the store," so we learned to not abuse the privilege. As a result, our parents were very generous in letting our friends share in our "candy wonderland." Our classmates and friends still remember and still talk about those good ol' days—and sleepless nights—when we would have sleepovers or "spend the night parties" in the attic at The Triangle.

LIFE LESSON NUMBER TEN

If you have a big empty space upstairs, it's better to do something with it.

CHAPTER ELEVEN

Bugs And Business As Usual

Having "grown up" in one, I have the greatest respect for people who work in grocery stores. Anyone with any such experience, particularly in the produce department, knows about bugs. Oh, sure, we've all seen Fear Factor, with its Madagascar hissing cockroaches, and if you've ever owned a computer, I'm sure you're aware of "bugs," sometimes known as viruses. That's not the kind of bugs I'm referring to.

At The Triangle, these critters were an integral part of our lives. They came in primarily on produce we sold in the store, and, finding easy access to the house as well, the little varmints wasted no time getting "up close and personal."

At first, they were the *big* ones—the cockroaches! They became so plentiful that sometimes we had to dodge them with our feet when we walked into a room. I remember the popping sound they made when we landed on one, making a mess we'd have to clean up.

Mother and Daddy had designated Tuesday night as our "family night at the movies," so every time we would go, the little monsters seemed to party in the darkness while we were away. When we would come home and flick on the lights, they would literally fly off the walls, sending my sister and me screaming and running for cover!

Although it was truly disgusting, we learned that there were just some things you couldn't change, and finally accepted them as a necessary evil of selling produce in a Mom and Pop store attached to the house.

Miraculously we somehow got rid of the big guys, only to have them replaced by the smaller but more insidious and fruitful water bug (sometimes known as the Croton bug). These little guys wouldn't even wait for the dark. They were absolutely shameless in their quest to take over the house and store. They eventually became so bold that they began creeping up the kitchen table legs while we were eating and hiding under the tablecloth.

We didn't know this was happening until one night Mother decided to replace our old tablecloth with a new one. We used oil cloth because it resisted spills and lasted a long time. I'm not sure why, but it was Mother's custom to simply place a new oilcloth over the old one. Over several months, we would have maybe an inch or so of oilcloth on the table. Unbeknownst to us, this had become a fertile breeding ground for those filthy little vermin, and when Mother pulled the last few layers off, I can only attempt to describe the carnage.

I had never seen my mother tap dance until that night. Entire colonies of water bugs were spewing across the floor as Mother discovered the infestation and flung that nasty bottom layer aside in an attempt to keep from being crawled on! I don't think any of us slept that night for fear that the remaining hordes would declare war on us in our sleep.

Eventually someone suggested a plan to Mother that was supposedly guaranteed to rid the house of this scourge. Combine equal parts of Eagle Brand (sweetened condensed) milk and boric acid, mix well, and place in small containers such as bottle caps around where bugs congregate or travel and, *presto!*

Although we had tried just about everything under the sun and were naturally skeptical, we decided to give it a try. Believe it or not, in two weeks, there was not a single water bug to be found anywhere!

Unfortunately, though, this was not the end of our bug problems. Anyone who knows anything at all about the Deep South has heard of the *pseudonopterous* insect sometimes called the flying ant, but better known as the common dreaded *termite*. These little insects just love warm humid weather, and thrive on tasty wooden structures such as old country stores like The Triangle.

There's an old story about a frog and a pan of hot water. Wisdom has it that, if you throw a frog into a pan of boiling water, he'll immediately hop out, unharmed. But if you place him in a pan of cold water and gradually heat it up, he'll be cooked before he knows what hit him.

I think the same principle could apply to termites and people. If people don't know termites are in the floor below them, and they wait until a foot crashes through a soft spot, they're already "cooked."

And so it was at The Triangle. It started with a creaking sound in the middle of the floor. Carpet was for rich people, so we never had any. We always put "linoleum rugs" down in the house, and when they got old and worn, we moved them into the store to "protect" the floor.

Not a good plan, in retrospect. Had the rug not been "protecting" the floor, we might have noticed the soft spots developing right before our eyes—and under our feet. In no time, the floor began to sway like a worn out dingy in a typhoon. *Termites!* Surely, this was the end of our livelihood. *Not!*

Instead, it was decided that we would go on the offensive and declare all out war on the invaders. I'm thinking, *Great; we'll close the store—at least for a little while—and take a break from store keeping. NOT!*

My father was a really smart guy, having made the local newspaper in high school on more than one occasion for making all "A's" on his report card. So, with the cunning of a military commander, he plotted his strategy. *We'll divide the floor in half, move everything to one side, serve customers over there while we tear out the floor and replace it, then shift to the other side and repeat the plan.*

After conferring with some other high level (termite) experts, Daddy was advised that he should consider making the floor concrete rather than running the risk of re-infestation and ultimately loss of the entire structure.

As with any military campaign, wars take unexpected turns, and so it was with ours. As the project got underway, the soldiers (ours) realized that the damage was more extensive and far reaching than we had thought. The entire floor had to be torn out at once! Now, I'm still thinking closure of the store at this point. *Not!*

With the speed and dedication of General Patton's Third Army, our men had the floor out in less than a day. They simultaneously constructed a set of steps for customers to descend the two or three feet down to bare dirt, allowing them to shop in "break neck" discomfort. Our spare ladders came in very handy, as, invariably, someone would request an item on the top shelf—by now far out of reach.

Later, we joked about the whole process, with such comments as, "Wow, this is truly a ground floor opportunity for us!" or "Now we can learn the grocery business from the ground up!"

In record time, preparation on the ground was completed, and the plan was to bring the truck in, pour the cement down the snout through the front door late in the evening, pray for a dry night, and "re-open" for business the next day. If I had never believed in miracles before, this was indeed my "conversion." Aside from a little inconvenience and having to endure a bit of "thigh-master" exercise, I don't think we missed a single customer during that time—truly a miracle!

And I'm sure the message was loud and clear to any potential, marauding termites: *Don't mess with The Triangle. You'll have to chew through concrete to get to the good stuff!*

LIFE LESSON NUMBER ELEVEN

When life "bugs" you, check your foundation first, then step out on it.

CHAPTER TWELVE

Saturday Morning At The Movies

I'm sure many books have been written about what we would call "the good old days," which included stories about the great cowboys such as Roy Rogers, Gene Autry, and Hopalong Cassidy. I saw many movies starring these great American "heroes," and, although I enjoyed them immensely, along with the likes of The Little Rascals and The Bowery Boys, I would be hard pressed to recall one single plot or story line from those movies.

What I do remember, however, is the wonderful times and the wonderful people that made those movie-going experiences unforgettable. The most significant of these was my maternal grandmother, whom we affectionately called "Mama Norman."

Mama Norman was a kind, gentle woman with thin black hair who wore tiny rimless glasses, dipped snuff, and was the consummate genteel grandmother. She married my grandfather when she was fifteen and he was thirty-five. The story goes that he had known her as a little girl, and had made the statement, "When she grows up, I'm going to marry her." And so he did. I was told that, back then, such a union was not that unusual.

My grandfather, Brock, was good to her, and they eked out a living on eighty acres of worn-out farm land and a couple of similarly worn out mules. Mama Norman always wore dresses, as was the custom for most women of her era, and I don't remember her ever driving a car. She was a lady in every sense of the word.

After we moved to The Triangle, we were much closer to "town," and all the excitement the little metropolis offered—including a "picture show" (aka, movie theater). It became a tradition on Saturday morning for Mama Norman to take my sister, Jean, and me to the movies. For the steep price of 15 cents (35 cents for anyone over the age of twelve), we got to see a double feature—usually a cowboy/western and a "murder mystery," coming attractions, a newsreel, a serial (a sort of continuing soap opera to get viewers to come back each week), and, best of all, a color cartoon!

We would get to the theater just before 10 A.M. and get out around 2 P.M., starving to death! But it was worth it, just to get to spend time with Mama Norman.

One interesting thing about the theater was its proximity to the Duck Inn, about two doors away. The Duck Inn was a little eatery where movie goers could get snacks before, during, and after the movie. The only "snack" one could purchase in the theater was a bag of popcorn popped in a portable machine just inside the "lobby." The job of popcorn popper was coveted, and often the springboard to more successful careers. It was common knowledge that our local sheriff, Delwin, had once been a popcorn popper at the theater.

The ancient, purple-haired lady who sold tickets knew everybody (if not by name, then by face), so you could wave to her as you left for the Duck Inn, scoot up there for some refreshments or goodies, and then re-enter the theater unchallenged. I never saw that purple-haired lady anywhere but in that ticket booth. As far as I knew, she lived there.

Those Saturdays were usually fairly uneventful, except for the change of plots in the movies. I gained quite a reputation for my raucous laughter during Dean Martin and Jerry Lewis movies or the antics of The Little Rascals. However, one seemingly normal Saturday morning suddenly took a turn for the worse when, during a particularly scary scene in one of the murder mysteries, I sucked a Life Saver down my throat gasping for the hero. At first, Mama Norman thought I was just excited about the movie as I began flailing my arms and alternately grabbing my throat and struggling for air. When I was finally able to choke out the words, *"I swallowed a Life Saver!"* Mama Norman hastily escorted my sister and me out of the theater. Did she perform the Heimlich? No, we simply raced over to Mr. Hamilton's grocery store about a half block away where she purchased a lemon for me to suck on. I later ate plenty of Life Savers, but never again during Saturday morning at the movies.

The years came and went, and the tradition we thought would continue forever added memory after wonderful memory to our lives. But then one day came the announcement that Mama Norman was sick, and the next Saturday would be the last time she would be taking Jean and me to the movies. And that was it. Somehow we knew this wasn't good, although we never really talked about it. In our family, you accepted things the way they were, and you didn't question why.

My grandmother died several months later, after a long and tortuous battle with colon cancer. And still today, when I see an old "picture show," I remember the good times Mama Norman, Jean and I shared on those unforgettable Saturday mornings at the movies.

LIFE LESSON NUMBER TWELVE

Movies are fun, but the drama of life is better.

CHAPTER THIRTEEN

Life Goes On At The Movies

Although it wasn't the same without Mama Norman, our mother was determined to keep the Saturday morning tradition alive. She would see to it that Jean and I made it to the picture show every Saturday, and gradually, we accepted the fact that life must go on.

Later we started another tradition of going to the movies every Tuesday night as a family—that is, if we could get the store closed in time. We didn't have regular store hours at The Triangle. The philosophy was, as long as paying customers were coming in, the store was open. And it almost never failed; when we would get ready to close the door and turn out the lights to enjoy a relaxing night at the movies, a car would drive up, invariably followed by three or four more. Sometimes we wouldn't make it at all, if too many customers showed up. We all learned to accept disappointment as an inevitable feature of movie-going. (I think I was well into my teens before I saw a movie from beginning to end without having to see the last part first!)

One such disappointment came following the announcement that the incredible Lash LaRue would be coming in person to our own little home town theater. This was at the height of the "Cowboy and Indian" movie craze, and all the kids were excited out of their minds!

I could name all of the cowboys during that time: Roy Rogers, Gene Autry, Wild Bill Elliot, The Cisco Kid, The Durango Kid, The Lone Ranger, Johnny Mack Brown, Whip Wilson, Hopalong Cassidy—the list goes on. But the thing that made these Westerns much more interesting was the main characters' "side kicks," who were usually hilariously funny buffoons who sometimes "saved the day" in spite of their idiocy. Each cowboy had his own: Roy Rogers had Gabby Hayes; Gene Autry had Smiley Burnette and Pat Buttram; Wild Bill Elliott had Andy Devine; and Lash LaRue had my favorite—Fuzzy St. John.

Lash LaRue himself was dashingly handsome—a sort of crude forerunner to the more polished Zorro—and could perform miracles with his famous bull whip. He could draw his whip out faster than any villain could draw his six-shooter, and disarm him at blinding speed. Why, we'd even seen ol' Lash pop a cigarette out of a cowpoke's mouth without even so much as grazing his nose!

And now he was coming in person. I don't know if anyone else wondered whether he would bring his side kick with him or not, but, in the movies, I'd never seen him without him, so I just assumed that he would be there too. It never occurred to me that they were two separate entities, and therefore would cost the promoters twice as much to have both of them come.

So, Lash LaRue's appearance with his famous whip, although exciting and enjoyable, was somewhat of a disappointment because I kept waiting for ol' Fuzzy to stumble in like he always did in the movies and bring the house down. (I did, however, get my own personally autographed picture of Lash LaRue out of the deal!)

Probably my most disappointing movie experience occurred one spring after I had seen the coming attractions for an "end-of-the-world" sci-fi movie featuring huge fire-breathing monsters and Godzilla-type reptiles. Each month, at the theater, patrons would receive a flyer showing all the movies to be shown for the upcoming month. I had seen the "ad" in the flyer, but didn't get really excited about it until I saw the "preview." It was to be shown on a Saturday (of course), and only on that day, so I began making plans to attend, telling all my friends to be sure and be there too. In those days in our small town, a movie would typically be shown for only one or two days, so if you missed it, you never got another chance to see it.

I eagerly anticipated this movie (I don't remember the name of it—only that it was about monsters and the end of the world) for what seemed like years. The week before the showing I noticed a strange tingling and swelling in my jaws, just below my ears. *Mumps!*

My life was over. Not from the mumps, but because I was convinced I would die if I didn't see that movie.

Well, I didn't see the movie, and obviously I didn't die, but that single event became the defining moment in my dealing with true disappointment. Life does go on.

LIFE LESSON NUMBER THIRTEEN

Life is full of disappointments, but it goes on anyway.

CHAPTER FOURTEEN

My Brush With A Movie Star

Besides the inevitable "disappointments" of movie-going as a young boy, the pastime had other hazards as well. To name a few, it was dark inside the theater, the aisles were strewn with spilled popcorn, slippery candy wrappers (from the Duck Inn), sticky chewing gum under the seats, and, worst of all, little girls!

My worst tormentor was a sweet, skinny, bright-eyed, bucktoothed darling named Elizabeth. Although I will not reveal her true identity, let's just say that, if you knew her last name, you would recognize it as a famous young and beautiful up-and-coming movie starlet of that era. But, in my mind, "little Liz" was the farthest thing from a movie star. In fact, if the truth be known, she was a downright *pest*.

It seemed that she was there, in the theater, every time I showed up, lurking in the shadows, waiting for a chance to pounce on me. She would then plop down in the seat next to mine and spend the next two to four hours lovingly clinging to my arm. Well, at that age, this just wasn't the thing to be caught having done to you. My little boy buddies would unmercifully taunt me when they would see little Liz chasing me up and down the aisles, and then clamp down on my arm as I sank lower and lower into my seat.

My favorite diversionary tactic was to tell little Liz that I had to go to the bathroom or get a drink of water, or *whatever*, then I would sneak back in and creep down the other aisle and take a seat as far away from my predator as I could get. No matter. Little Liz would always find me and the scenario would repeat itself until I would finally give up and submit to the humiliation of spending *eternity* with a girl in a dark, God-forsaken place.

I eventually came to accept little Liz as a part of my life, however, and was even known to be seen with her on occasion outside of the movie theater. By the time we made it to the fifth grade, it was understood that if boys and girls participated in *anything* in which you had to have a partner, little Liz and I would end up together. One of those excruciating events was Miss Madie's Fifth Grade Dance Recital with me in my "Sunday best" and little Liz in her "gown," complete with doily headpiece and wrist corsage!

Although I never really claimed *her*, she never gave up on me until we finally graduated from grammar school. This milestone culminated in what was known as the Sixth Grade Banquet, and you guessed it. Elizabeth, of course, asked me to go with her, and, since I had never refused her (it never did any good anyway!), I accepted reluctantly.

She and her Aunt Sara picked me up at The Triangle, and we were escorted to the "banquet hall" where we were able to demonstrate our dancing acumen left over from Miss Madie's recital the previous year.

As my grammar school career came to an end, and shortly after the aforementioned banquet, another significant event took place in my life. Near the very end of the school year, I unexpectedly began experiencing nausea and malaise to the point where I literally couldn't get out of bed. After several days of this, I was admitted to our little hospital where I was diagnosed with food poisoning, or intestinal flu, or bronchial pneumonia, or something like that.

Actually, I'm not convinced now that it wasn't just the onset of puberty, because after several days in the hospital, I began to find the strength to sit up in bed, and something really strange began to happen. I found myself drawn to the window of my room which, coincidentally, was adjacent to Elizabeth's back yard.

The day before I was released from the hospital, I remember swinging my feet over the edge of the bed, looking out the window, and seeing Elizabeth and her friend Eleanor frolicking in her back yard. Now, understand, that prior to this particular day, I was aware only that the main difference between boys and girls was that girls sometimes had longer hair. But today...I felt strangely compelled to admire Elizabeth's legs, which were marvelously visible due to her newly-donned spring shorts. I didn't know what had hit me, but I somehow knew that my life as a "little boy" would never be the same.

Apparently I wasn't the only little boy who was experiencing this strange metamorphosis because, from that day on, the only time I saw Elizabeth was with a throng of boys chasing *her!* It seemed that, overnight, she had grown from a pesky, skinny little girl to a beautiful young lady who had no use for the little boy she had once chased down the aisles at the "picture show."

Although I never got the chance to officially "date" beautiful Elizabeth, I admired her from afar, as boyfriend after boyfriend fell prey to her charm. She eventually fell in love, married, and had a family, and a successful career in education as a teacher and principal of a nearby high school. Sadly, she was taken from us when she lost her battle with cancer just a few years ago.

Many years after Elizabeth and I parted ways, I still remember her fondly, and regret that I never got the chance to tell her how much she impacted my life early on, and how close she was to being "my brush with a movie star."

LIFE LESSON NUMBER FOURTEEN

The biggest movie stars in Hollywood can't touch us like the stars in our own life.

CHAPTER FIFTEEN

The Drive-In Comes To Town

There's an old saying which goes, "All good things must come to an end." And so it was with the "picture show" in town. During the time the Drive-In was taking over the movie-viewing business, the indoor theater became known as the "Walk-In." Eventually, it became a casualty of progress as the "younger crowd" found a safe haven at the Drive-In for smooching and necking in the privacy of their cars.

Still, change was hard for movie-goers in our little town, and no one really expected the Drive-in to make it. On opening night, there was to be a fireworks display, but even this wasn't much of a draw. I didn't care anything about seeing the movie, but I did want to see the fireworks (I'd never seen one except maybe in movies, and I'd shot a few firecrackers and lit some sparklers).

So Daddy and I drove the three or four miles to the Drive-In and parked across the road from the giant screen, which was clearly visible for a good quarter mile either way. We didn't know the fireworks were scheduled *after* the movie, so we spent most of that night chatting with cheapskate curiosity seekers looking for a free thrill, most of whom didn't have the patience to wait through a two-hour movie to watch a few fireworks go off. Nevertheless, Daddy and I hung in there, and, as fireworks displays of that era go, it probably wasn't that bad. It just wasn't worth having to struggle through a silent movie to see it.

Eventually we came to accept the new Drive-In as a vital part of the entertainment scene in our little community. Long before my sister and I got our driver's licenses, we would get various relatives to take us out for a night at the Drive-In. Our favorites were Uncle Doc and Aunt Dycia. However, we paid a dear price by going with them, because both were heavy smokers. During the winter months, it was a choice between freezing or suffocating. During many a movie, Jean and I would alternate cracking the windows in the back seat and sticking our noses out to suck in some blessed fresh air before the orders would come, "Roll up that window! It's gettin' cold in here!" Oh, the price we had to pay for family togetherness!

Just as the Walk-In succumbed to the Drive-In, eventually the Drive-In gave up the ghost to a young upstart entertainment medium called television, and soon families were staying home watching free "movies" in the comfort of their living rooms.

As budding adolescents, most of us kids began to seek other avenues of socialization. Surprisingly, for such a small town, our community boasted several. Happy Days had Arnold's, but long before that (before Opie even appeared in Mayberry), we had Ed's, which became *the* place to be on every weekend night. It featured plenty of "parking" space for young people to meet, greet, and eat. It even had "car hops" who came out to take our orders. Two other popular hangouts were favorite haunts of local youngsters. One was the Dairy *Dream*, our forerunner to today's Dairy *Queen.*

The Dairy Dream had been around for a while and had opened with much hoopla, featuring this new-fangled "soft serve ice milk." On opening day, it almost caused a riot when all the buses from the grammar school and high school stopped after school so the kids could get a free sample of this tasty new treat.

The other "place to be" was a local boat-factory-turned-skating-rink, complete with a full-sized rink and a kiddy rink for the little ones. There were even a couple of bowling alleys inside the big building, and money could be earned as a pin setter if a young boy had the nerve. The job was quite dangerous, as most folks in town had never seen a bowling alley or bowling ball, and would often hurl the shiny black "cannonballs" down the alley before the brave (or foolish!) young pin setter could jump out of the way.

During the time all of these attractions were at their peak, the Drive-In, in an effort to compete for business, showed a scandalous movie called "The Miracle of Birth." All the kids tried to keep it a secret from their parents because they knew it would be absolutely forbidden for them to see it. When it was shown, I bummed a ride with some older friends—all of us, of course, telling our parents we were going to the skating rink.

Although quite graphic, the movie was a huge disappointment, and hardly worth the guilt we all felt for lying to our parents to see a cheap "pornographic" movie. After the movie, we all converged on the skating rink about the same time, only to be met by a good many of our parents who had gotten wind of our plans. My father was waiting for me, and not a word was said as we drove quietly home. I guess he figured the humiliation of the moment was punishment enough. To my knowledge, there was never another movie of that "caliber" shown at the Crenshaw Drive-In Theater.

LIFE LESSON NUMBER FIFTEEN

It's not always <u>what</u> your parents say that's important; sometimes it's what they <u>don't</u> say that you appreciate.

CHAPTER SIXTEEN

Trauma: Life In Our E.R.

I learned early on that, not only disappointment, but also tragedy and death were a normal part of life. It seemed that, in our family, there was always something happening that required good coping skills and a strong will.

My paternal grandfather, "Daddy Moody," had leukemia, and died while having a checkup in the doctor's office. When he died, it was the first time I had ever seen my father cry. My maternal grandfather died shortly thereafter of a heart attack. Both were in their seventies. Except for Mama Norman, who died of cancer in her forties, the women in our family usually outlived the men.

Such deaths seemed to "cluster" themselves together. My grandfathers died within two weeks, and my paternal grandmother and her sister-in-law, my great aunt Nina, who lived with her, died during Christmas week one year. We had quite a large extended family, and there were many elderly great aunts, uncles, and cousins who passed away during my childhood. My mother's side of the family seemed to suffer the most, with cancer claiming many lives.

One of the most tragic was Mother's brother, Carl, whom we affectionately called "Doc." He and his brother, Raymond, were soldiers in World War II. Doc made it home, but unfortunately Raymond was killed. Doc was a robust, fun-loving man with curly blond hair and dancing blue eyes. He drove a truck for a living, and was always "kidding around." In fact, most of the time we couldn't tell when he was joking or when he was serious.

One of his favorite things to do was to wrestle with us kids. Sometimes his roly poly stomach would pop out, and he'd shout, gesturing toward his belly button, "Watch out! That's where the Yankee shot me!" As kids, we didn't know one war from another, so he actually had us believing some sort of "Northerner" had wounded him with a musket. It didn't matter that we all had belly buttons!

But then came the diagnosis that tested his happy-go-lucky spirit to the limit. It was colon cancer, and the prognosis was not good. The surgery and ensuing treatment eventually left him thin and gaunt, a shadow of the man he once was.

In spite of his uncertain future, Doc went on with his life, and one day showed up at our door with his bride-to-be, Dycia. She was beautiful in her yellow chiffon dress, and we were all happy for Doc. Knowing he was dying, she married him and bore two children, first Glenna, and, a year later, Raymond.

After months of suffering, Doc passed away when Raymond was two years old. Dycia never remarried, but devoted her life to caring for her two children. Caring for Doc in his final months afforded Dycia the opportunity to learn, first hand and "on the job," how to be a nurse. That training with her beloved Doc led, years later, to an RN degree, which helped her support her family. Doc always wanted to be able to provide for them, and, indeed, he did.

Glenna and Raymond were several years younger than Jean and me, so we spent many hours "baby sitting" and playing with what seemed like our own sister and brother. One day, when Glenna was just a few months old, we were "showing her off" to some customers who had come into the store. I'm not sure which one of us was actually holding her, but she hadn't yet learned to walk, so we were letting her do some "leg exercises" on top of the counter next to the cash register. Bouncing like the proverbial rubber ball, suddenly she went airborne, and in a split second was plummeting head first to the floor! Although it knocked the wind out of her, it took only a couple of seconds for her to sound off! It was music to our ears, and other than a nice goose bump on top of her head, she was O.K.

A couple of years later, Raymond wasn't so fortunate. Dycia's parents had a sort of Mom and Pop store a few miles to the west, just outside of the town of Rutledge, called The Big Apple (a far cry from

New York City!). Glenna and Raymond had a large "playground" out front which, unfortunately, they had to share with all the cars and trucks that stopped by daily for gas and a few quick groceries. As one of the customers backed out, he ran squarely over Raymond's legs, breaking both of them. The little fellow hadn't been walking very long, and now had two full casts on his legs.

As if that weren't bad enough, because of his tender age, the legs healed quickly—but crooked—and had to be re-broken and re-set. He was in traction and had to lie on his back for several weeks. He was just learning to talk, and everyone who visited the little tyke and tended to him talked "baby talk" to him. It was literally years before he learned to speak "adult" English.

And let's not leave out the story of Jean's appendectomy. During her recovery, she had an allergic reaction to penicillin and had to be rushed to the hospital. Our local hospital had only about eight or ten beds and one room for maternity patients. You guessed it. All the beds were full except the "maternity ward," and that's where she ended up. It took about nine months to quell the rumor!

And finally, there was my tonsillectomy. I had had earaches, sore throats, colds, and sinus problems for years. I have suspected that my propensity for infection may have contributed, at least partly, to my hearing loss. I had contracted measles and had a horrendous earache for several days. The doctors said the measles "settled" in my left ear, and when it was all over, I was totally deaf in that ear. The explanation was that the cilia in my cochlea had been destroyed, making it impossible for the sound "signal" to be transmitted to my brain. My right ear was not affected, and I eventually learned to adapt.

Finally, my parents decided it was time to take my tonsils and adenoids out, because that's apparently where a lot of my problems originated. It was decided that we would wait until I was fairly healthy to schedule the surgery. All my friends thought I was lying the night I showed up at a local baseball game and announced I was getting my tonsils out the next morning.

We arrived at the hospital in Troy, about twenty miles away, around 7 A.M., and were met in the hallway by a nurse who gave me a pill to take before going into my room. A few minutes later, the "dope" began to take effect, and I was fighting off sleep as they wheeled me into the cold, bright operating room. As they strapped my arms down, I felt a needle stick my arm.

About a half second later (it seemed) I was begging for water, with the worst sore throat I had ever had! It was actually 24 hours later, and for the next six days, I ate Jell-O and soup, thinking that this whole tonsillectomy thing was a mistake. I woke up the morning before my one-week checkup with the "sniffles," rose up on one elbow, and filled my hand with blood pouring from my nose. Mother called the doctor, and was told that, apparently, I had "pulled the scab off" in my sleep. The next day, he gave me a "clean bill," and told me I could eat anything I wanted. Across the street from the hospital was a pastry shop called the Troy Maid Bakery. Mother took me over there and bought me a sack full of donuts. Although it still hurt to swallow, I ate donuts all the way home—my first solid food in a week.

I had several other "run-ins" with doctors throughout my childhood, including a broken collar bone, a broken arm (trying to pull a weed out of the front wheel of my bicycle—while riding it!), bronchial pneumonia, food poisoning, intestinal flu, and numerous cuts with knives and broken glass, in addition to all of the usual childhood maladies such as measles, mumps, and chicken pox.

And so it went in *our* E.R. Nothing you could make a TV series out of, but certainly significant enough to fill our lives full of stories that have been told countless times.

LIFE LESSON NUMBER SIXTEEN

Life without trauma is non-existent; without trauma, life is just existence.

CHAPTER SEVENTEEN

Gender Roles: Stepping Outside The Box

Growing up with an older sister, I often had difficulty learning about "gender roles." I figured if my sister, Jean, could do it, so could I, not knowing that certain things are just not done by boys. I had gotten a little taste of this when I would "inherit" her bicycles as hand-me-downs, and get kidded for riding them. (See Chapter Six.) And, I liked playing with dolls and wearing soft pastel colors.

We've come a long way since then, and I'm glad. Even though I still believe there are certain things that the sexes should be pigeon-holed into (like only men working in a men's prison), I actually feel exonerated in the 21st century having had those "girly" preferences as a child.

One of my best friends in elementary school was Marvin, a blond-haired, blue-eyed little tyke who was the first to teach me it was O.K. to think outside the box on gender issues. Marvin and I met in the third grade. He just showed up in class one day, and was immediately "noticeable." His hair was always tousled, and he had a laid-back manner that made those of us who were already friends want to make him part of our gang right off the bat. Marvin stayed with us for only a couple of years, but made a lasting impression on all of us. One of his eyelids was "lazy" and drooped noticeably. He never said anything about it, but we all wondered about Marvin's eye. Marvin was not an athletic kid, and liked a lot of the things I did, so we soon became fast friends.

One day, my curiosity got the best of me, and I popped the question. "Marvin, what's wrong with your eye?"

He looked at me incredulously, and with an air of confidence that made me feel like something was wrong with *my* eye, replied, "There's nothing wrong with my eye."

And that was the end of it. It was obvious that he was aware of it and probably somewhat sensitive about it. But he also must have been taught to not be ashamed of it and not make a big deal out of it.

So, I never brought it up again, and word must have gotten around, because nobody else ever brought it up either. As far as I know, nobody ever found out what was wrong with Marvin's eye. The next time I had a question for Marvin, I was a little less blunt, and a little more tactful.

Then one day I noticed something else about Marvin that was "different." It was his fingernails. I'm not sure what made me first notice that they were sort of "shiny." Again, my curiosity got the best of me, but I approached him with guarded trepidation this time.

"Marvin…I've noticed that your…fingernails…they're kinda shiny…"

Raising one eyebrow (not the one with the sleepy lid), he sidled closer and glanced from side to side, as if checking for eavesdroppers, and whispered, "It's fingernail polish."

I was shocked. "No, it's not," I retorted, "fingernail polish is *red*."

With a sly grin and an air of confidence reminiscent of his eyelid declaration weeks earlier, he stated, "Naw, it comes in clear, too."

"Oh, yeh?" I replied, amazed. Now it's my turn to check for eavesdroppers, as *I* sidle closer. "Can you get me some?"

"Sure," Marvin boasts, "I'll bring you some tomorrow."

And thus began my deep, but short-lived, love affair with clear fingernail polish. Once I got it out of my system and the mystique was gone, I abandoned the idea that boys would ever be considered normal if they wore fingernail polish. I understand that, today, some men actually get manicures, as well as pedicures. Can we say, "…outside the box?"

LIFE LESSON NUMBER SEVENTEEN

Stepping "outside the box" requires coming "full circle" in your thinking.

CHAPTER EIGHTEEN

Some Final Lessons

To say that my pre-teen years were turbulent and unsettling would be an understatement. Everything was changing—my body, my social life, my school environment. One of the least visible changes, but one of the most significant ones was my mind. It was expanding. And absorbing. And processing. I remember, vividly, significant issues that would just "come upon me" without warning. One of the most profound occurred while playing with my dog in the back yard one bright, clear spring day after school. My pets, particularly my dogs, were an important part of my life as a child. I was into Ol' Yeller, Lassie, Rin Tin Tin, Rex the Wonder Dog, Beautiful Joe, and every mutt and cur that wandered up into our yard. I must have been a natural-born caretaker, as I lost count of the number of dogs I rescued from certain starvation and death during my growing-up years.

I'm not sure which one of those little mutts had attacked my foot, causing me to fall into the cool grass. Fido (I'll call him) was playfully "going in for the kill," biting me unmercifully around my face and neck. As I was fighting him off, there was a lull in the attack, and, flat on my back, I opened my eyes and came face to face with the concept of infinity. Previously I had thought of things as having a beginning and an end, a start and a finish. Suddenly, I realized for the first time, that there was no end to the clear blue sky I was gazing into.

For several minutes, I lay there, amazed that I had never known this before. *How was this possible? If you keep going out there, what would you run into? How did we get here?* The questions were rapid fire, and endless. My mother had always seen to it that we attended Sunday School and church every Sunday, and this part of my life often conflicted with the secular teachings I received in school. If the story of Adam and Eve was true, then where did Neanderthal and Cro-Magnon man fit in, I questioned. Thus began a search for knowledge as to the "meaning of life" which continues to this day.

Many other, less profound, lessons were picked up along the way. In our school, the first through twelfth grades were all within a 200 yard radius, and my assumption, early on, was that all the grades would be equally "manageable." When I entered the seventh grade, however, my education *really* started. No longer was it memorization of facts and figures. Now it was *experiencing* life. Like, for example, my first trip to the library, and being addressed, "Hey, *little boy*." A few months earlier, I was a sixth grade "upper classman!" This experience taught me that people can be cruel without meaning to be.

Then there was the day I was approached by Jimmy, an older boy who demanded that I give him some candy I had in my pocket. When I refused, he struck me in the back, knocking me face down onto the gymnasium floor. As I slid across the floor, I heard his laughter and that of his friends burning in my ears. This taught me that some people can be cruel *intentionally*.

Even as a child, I had always been rather fastidious about my appearance. Good grooming was imperative, and I believed in having "every hair in place." One popular product of the day that helped me with that was Avon Hair Trainer, an early forerunner to today's styling mousse and spritz. The stuff came in a small red plastic bottle, and was available only through a friend of my mother's who sold Avon on the side to make some extra cash. Once it was applied and the hair combed into place, it stayed there. Except when my nemesis, Quitman Thatcher, zeroed in on me in the hallway. It was his mission in life to mess up my hair, and he did it almost daily for months—maybe years. My experience with Quitman taught me the Serenity Prayer (before I knew what it really meant): *God grant me the serenity to accept the things I cannot change, courage to change the things I can, and the wisdom to know the difference.* I'll bet if ol' Quitman is still around, he's still messing up somebody's hair!

I don't know how my Civics teacher would feel about this next revelation. I'm not sure if I just learned one thing in his class, or if the lesson I learned was so significant that all else paled in comparison. It was the concept of limited freedom with responsibility. The teacher put it this way: *The freedom to swing my fist ends where your nose begins.* This principle has been applied in my life ever since that day it made such a deep impression on me.

And then there was the lesson in anger management I learned from my school bus driver, "Miss Thelma." She was a sweet mild-mannered genteel Southern lady who was always the same, no matter what the circumstances. Because she was such a "class act," and the kids loved and respected her so much, it never occurred to any of us to misbehave on her bus.

It was customary for all of the buses to congregate around the school in no particular order. When the final bell rang, there was a mad dash for the buses, with each kid racing to get the front seat on the bus. Then, again, in no particular order, the buses would pull out as soon as we were aboard. Rules of the road were observed, and the Golden Rule always applied, of course. In such a small town, if *any* rule of *any* kind was violated, it was a major event, because, by sundown, everybody in town knew about it.

I don't remember who the culprit was, but one of the buses lurched ahead of our bus, causing Miss Thelma to have to slam on her brakes and swerve to avoid a collision. Since she was the only female bus driver at that time (another one of those rare gender role violations), I've often wondered if this was an intentional act to show Miss Thelma who was "the boss." Although no real harm was done, we were all a little shaken, and I will never forget Miss Thelma's reaction. After a slight pause to compose herself, she let the world know she was p***ed off. With almost no expression and in a barely audible voice, she muttered, "Ooo, that makes me so angry."

That was the "maddest" I ever saw Miss Thelma. Come to think of it, that was the *only* time I ever saw Miss Thelma angry. I remember wondering, if that's what it's like to be angry, why can't everybody be that way? In group therapy sessions years later, I have often related

Miss Thelma's "angry outburst" story to illustrate that anger management is indeed possible.

Perhaps my most memorable lesson in the "social graces" was taught to me by my English teacher, "Miss Evelyn," as I was returning to fourth period class from lunch. It had been a fairly good day, and I was feeling pretty good about myself. I was walking down the sidewalk, and unbeknownst to me, followed by Miss Evelyn. The door to the building had a long flight of stairs which led up to it. Just before ascending the stairs, I caught a glimpse of Miss Evelyn about 15 or 20 steps behind me. Now, I knew the rule. Always, *always*, hold the door open for a lady. But this was no lady; this was *Miss Evelyn*—more than a lady—so the rule applied even more so. However, my computer brain must have been processing slowly that day. Let's consider the factors: (1) I was running a little late for class, (2) I was a good distance ahead of Miss Evelyn (Is there a "distance rule" here?), (3) although I had seen Miss Evelyn, I wasn't sure she'd seen me (not a good excuse), and (4) I might've been lazy (a better excuse). All these things considered, the decision was made. I accelerated, taking the stairs three at a time, and slipped through the door, allowing it to ease shut behind me.

In retrospect, I honestly believe Miss Evelyn planned, from that second on, to make an example of me in her sixth period English class. We were scarcely seated when Miss Evelyn chortled, "I'd like everyone to know that young Mr. Moody here does not yet know that he is supposed to *always* hold the door for a lady (pause for effect). Isn't that right, Mike?" There had been times in my life when I had felt lonely and alone, but none of those times compared to this one, on the front row of Miss Evelyn's class with all eyes upon me. "Yes, ma'am," I answered weakly. And as if this weren't enough, she related the entire incident in graphic detail, much to the delight of my fellow classmates.

Some lessons are "hard learned." That was not one of them. To this day, I *always* hold a door for a lady. Thank you, Miss Evelyn.

LIFE LESSON NUMBER EIGHTEEN

There's a life lesson behind every door; hold it open as long as you can.

CHAPTER NINETEEN

Santa Claus And Slot Machines

Although I don't remember actually living on the farm, I do remember my parents talking to me about how life on the farm was—and how certain things would not be the same after we moved off of it and bought The Triangle. In their opinion, life would be better for us. However, I wasn't so sure. One of the things I definitely had a problem with was the fact that our "new" home had no fireplaces and, therefore, no chimneys. Well, this didn't really bother me at first, because we moved to The Triangle in January. But it started to bother me as the year wore on toward fall and winter, and I began to wonder how Santa Claus was going to get in! My mother had assured me that the old man didn't have to come down a chimney; she explained that we'd just leave the door unlocked and he could come in that way. Another "fly in the ointment," though, was the fact that my father had gotten into the slot machine business.

I guess Las Vegas had always been around, but I'm sure the gambling Mecca in Biloxi, Mississippi was not even a twinkle in developers' eyes when we got our first "one-armed bandit" at The Triangle. We had lived in Columbus, Georgia (just across the Chattahoochee River from Phenix City, Alabama) with one of Daddy's cousins for about six months before we moved to The Triangle. Having a farm background, Daddy worked for the Agricultural Adjustment Agency ("The Triple A," as we called it) in Phenix City, but things hadn't worked out, so we moved back to Crenshaw County. I think Phenix City must be where Daddy got the idea to put slot machines in our store. A movie called The Phenix City Story, about the mess over there came out in 1955, depicting this sleepy post-World War II Alabama town after it was taken over by the Mob. It was all about the crooked gambling, loan sharking, and prostitution directed at the soldiers at Ft. Benning, Georgia, just across the state line.

All that going on over there was probably part of the reason we left, but we apparently took part of it with us. No sooner had we gotten the addition put on the store, when a big flashy slot machine showed up in that back room. There weren't really any laws governing the use of them back then, or, if there were, nobody paid any attention to them. In addition to the big one, we had a couple of smaller slot machines that took only nickels, and worked like a coin-operated washing machine at a laundromat. Sometimes I would sneak some change out of the cash register and try my hand at the machines. I still remember the thrill of hitting the jackpot! It's a wonder I didn't get addicted to gambling at that early age. Mother didn't really like the fact that we had them, but she was from the "old school," and usually supported whatever Daddy implemented at The Triangle.

As the day inched toward December 25th, the crowds in that back room got bigger—and stayed later—undoubtedly looking for the big break that would help them pay off some of their Christmas bills. Even though I had played the machines myself, somehow I knew they weren't "a good thing," and worried that if Santa Claus came, he would be disgusted at the sight of all those men smoking, cursing, shouting, and wagering, and surely pass us by.

Mother, however, was the consummate comforter and arbiter, and assured me again that they would be gone by the time Santa made his rounds. I went to sleep that night in my bedroom next to the "casino" not knowing whether I would be blessed with Santa's presence or not. But, true to her word, Mother apparently ran the rascals off, and Christmas morning was unforgettable. I don't remember what the gifts were; I just remember that Santa showed up as promised. It was our first Christmas with slot machines.

I never knew if "the heat" got too close, or if it was Mother who laid the law down about getting rid of them, but one day the one-armed bandits disappeared, never to rob again at The Triangle.

LIFE LESSON NUMBER NINETEEN

If you gamble on Santa Claus, you always win.

CHAPTER TWENTY

Last Name?....What Last Name?

In a small community like I grew up in, everybody knew everybody on a first name basis. In fact, last names were so unimportant that they were usually only used for legal purposes and such as that. Even people who were not close friends of my parents referred to them as "Mr. John" and "Miss Lillie." And, even though kids knew their school teachers' last names, it was perfectly permissible and acceptable to call them by their first names such as "Miss Ann" or "Miss Evelyn."

I was so unaware of last names when I was a little boy, that I just assumed I didn't have one. But thanks to one of the locals who was a regular customer at The Triangle, I found out one day that I did, indeed, have one.

The customer's nickname was "Pal" (I didn't find out until years later what his real name was), and he and his family had grown up right around The Triangle. He was somewhat of a kidder, especially with the kids in the neighborhood, and always seemed like everybody's "pal" (probably, hence, the name). He was a good bit older than me, and I thought he looked *much* older because he was almost totally bald.

Pal came into the store one day not too long after we had moved there, and caught me scurrying around trying to get away from my sister.

"Hey, boy, what's your name?" he asked.

After several weeks of having people walk into our grocery-laden living room, I had learned that no one is a stranger, so I quickly answered, "Mike."

"Oh, yeh?" Pal responded. "Mike *what?*"

Well, no one had ever asked me that question before. I figured he ought to know that I didn't have a last name, so I gave him a "smart" answer.

"Well, *Nothin',*" I replied, incredulously.

"Oh, Mike Nothin', huh? Your name is Mike Nothin'?" he chortled.

From that day on, I became known to my tormentor as "Mike Nothin'," and every time he saw me, he'd always salute me, "There's ol' Mike Nothin'!"

Of course, I found out later that *everybody* had last names, so not to be outdone, I started addressing him the same way. "There's ol' Pal Nothin'!"

Fortunately, the label didn't "warp" either of us, and I came to realize, not only that everybody has last names, but nobody is named "Nothin'!"

LIFE LESSON NUMBER TWENTY

If you're ever going to be somebody, don't think of yourself as "Nothin'."

CHAPTER TWENTY-ONE

Daisy Gets Caught Stealing

I have always believed in the power of knowledge (after getting over the initial shock of the first grade!), and am very grateful to have had the opportunity to obtain different types of education from several different schools. However, I also believe that the best education one can receive is from "The School of Hard Knocks."

Thus was the case with Daisy. Sometime after we moved to The Triangle in 1947 and Mother quit her job at the "sewing factory" to devote full time to parenting and store keeping, we "hired" Daisy. Daisy was a colored woman who lived about a half mile down the road from The Triangle with her family, which consisted of a husband and several children and grandchildren, crammed into a rundown clapboard house several yards off the main drag. She was the matriarch of her brood, and the one who worked "steady." My sister, Jean, and I immediately liked her. She probably wasn't even five feet tall, and was always laughing and smiling about something. She was very "hot-natured," and was most known for her complaint (when the temperature went over about 60 degrees), "It's hot, whoo-ee!"

In the days of the Old South, it wasn't uncommon to find any number of "colored folks" to do any number of odd jobs, and for a very low wage. We'd never heard of minimum wage, because back then, almost *all* wages were minimum. The pay was usually determined by "whatever the traffic would bear." I remember someone mentioning that a dollar a day was a pretty decent wage (this was when ground beef was around 50 cents a pound, gasoline was 25 cents a gallon, and cigarettes about the same price). Plus, if you added perks, such as a bag of left over biscuits and a piece of fatback, it was considered a "right good deal." Still, it was hard for most colored folks to make ends meet, and often we would see children scrounging and begging for food by asking, "Mama say you got 'nythang." In other words, "Mother sent us here to ask you if you have any food you could give us."

I'm not sure how long Daisy had been working for us, but it was long enough for us to believe she was a trusted employee. She definitely earned her meager salary, doing anything from cooking, cleaning, stocking shelves in the store, washing dishes and clothes, raking the yard, and even rocking Jean and me to sleep if necessary. However, one day Mother detected something odd about Daisy's behavior. Normally a heavy coat was out of the question for her, as she was always "hot." But this particular day, she kept her coat on, and Mother noticed her making several trips outside for no apparent reason. Hoping her suspicions were ill-founded, she watched from the kitchen window as Daisy made one of her treks to the back yard. Immediately her fears were confirmed as she observed Daisy pulling out several items concealed under her coat and hiding them in some nearby bushes.

Not one to mince words when it came to protecting her property, Mother confronted Daisy as she came back inside. "Daisy, I know what you're doing. Don't ever steal from me again. Go out and get that stuff you took and bring it back. If you ever need anything, just ask me for it, but don't ever steal from me again."

I'm amazed to think how times have changed. If that had happened today, the police would be called, an arrest would be made, charges filed, and several lawyers would be involved. The perpetrator would be fired, and would probably file a racial discrimination lawsuit, and the only beneficiaries would be the lawyers. Not to mention the betrayal of trust, and the loss of a beloved "member" of our family. I'm not minimizing the obvious discrimination, prejudice, and inequities Negroes endured during the 40's and 50's, but something has definitely gone awry.

Daisy never again stole anything (from us or from anyone else, so far as we know), and devotedly worked for our family long after that incident until her death many years later. She has been missed terribly, and is remembered fondly by all who knew her.

LIFE LESSON NUMBER TWENTY-ONE

You don't have to steal material things to steal someone's heart.

CHAPTER TWENTY-TWO

Target Practice With The BB Gun

When I was growing up, every little boy's greatest desire (at least those who lived in "the country") was to have a Red Ryder BB gun. Well, I finally got one. Unfortunately, it didn't come with instructions on how to shoot it. I did learn how to load it, and it was fully loaded and ready for target practice when my friend, Jimmy, showed up one night at the store. We sold a lot of cigarettes at The Triangle, and always had an ample supply of empty cigarette cartons (and other "pasteboard" boxes) waiting to be "recycled" as toys...or on this particular evening as targets for BB gun shooters. Unbeknownst to me, Jimmy, being about three years older, was an expert marksman. I had gathered an assortment of those cigarette cartons, and asked Jimmy if he'd like to join me in some showin' off target practice. Of course, being the crack shot he was, he agreed, knowing that it wouldn't be hard to show me up.

So, I proceeded to set up the first target on the arm of the old glider we had in front of the store—unfortunately right in front of four large pane-glass windows. We took turns on this makeshift firing range, taking pot shots at the (for me) elusive cigarette carton. I doubt we were more than six or eight feet from the target, and, for an expert like Jimmy who knew how to shoot, i.e., "aim" down the barrel, it was a bull's eye every time. And down would go the target. My frustration mounted with each hit by Jimmy and each miss by me. Finally, after what seemed like a hundred times on my part to try to score a hit, I exclaimed to Jimmy, "I bet I can't even hit that window!"

You guessed it. Jimmy left quickly to escape my mother's harsh tongue-lashing and my feeble attempt at explanation as to why I had scored a perfect hit right in the middle of that previously unadulterated window pane.

The last time I saw the old store, that perfect hit was still evident for everyone to see at the end of the "firing range."

LIFE LESSON NUMBER TWENTY-TWO

Sometimes you hit the target, even when you're not aiming for it.

CHAPTER TWENTY-THREE

Shooting Rats In The Kitchen

Before the days of Orkin and other pest control companies, there were rat traps, D-Con, and "22 rifles." As a child, I watched Mickey, Minnie, and Mighty Mouse in cartoons at the "Walk-In" theater in town. (It had to be at the theater, as we didn't get a TV until I was about eleven years old.) I had heard people talk about "mice" all of my young life, but in those days, regardless of size, we called all of them "rats." The bigger versions were known as wharf rats, and they were *big.* That's the kind that would show up in the store at The Triangle and in our house. It's not that we lived in squalor; it was just accepted as a part of life that, once in a while, we would encounter our friends, the wharf rats. They would usually find their way inside through a pipe, hidden cracks in the floors or walls, or maybe in a box of "produce" destined for sale in the store.

It was unusual for me to be at the store with just my father, because, in his younger days, to put it kindly, Daddy liked staying *away* from home more than staying *at* home and "keeping store," as we called it. Very few things, other than a death in the family, kept the store from being open in those days, and I knew, even as a child, that it was an important—and necessary—part of our lives. I later learned that it was responsible for paying most of our bills, because Daddy spent most of his salary on booze in the early days. Still, I didn't like working in the store. Nevertheless, one quiet night, my mother and sister had gone somewhere and left me to keep store with Daddy, and, as usual, I was looking for reasons to get out of it. After all, Daddy was a pretty good store keeper when he wanted to be, so while he was making small talk with one of our regular customers, I snuck into the kitchen to get something to eat. The kitchen was adjacent to the rear of the store, and, because my mother was the world's greatest cook, she always kept it stocked with special things to eat. Even the leftovers were good. I had a voracious appetite growing up, so the kitchen was one of my favorite places.

Little did I know that, as I stepped through the door separating the store from the kitchen, I would have some competition from "Mighty Mouse." His sheer size stopped me dead in my tracks, and at first glance, I had to rub my eyes to make sure I wasn't "seeing things." Ol' Mighty was sitting on his haunches, munching on who knows what, taken from who knows where (I didn't want to know), and as he turned toward me, our eyes locked. Apparently he had been feasting for some time, because as he ambled off, he literally wobbled from side to side! Rather than being frightened, he (I assumed, since it was so big, that it was a "he") seemed merely bothered that I had invaded *his* domain.

My about face and exit were quite rapid, and I excitedly announced to Daddy, "Th...Th...There's a rat in the kitchen!"

Daddy's response was just as rapid. Without hesitation, he barked his orders, military style. "Shut the door, and run around and shut the bedroom door so he can't get out!" And then the chilling words, "I'll get the rifle."

I guess he must have thought this rat was a big one, and no job for sissies. Some years before, Daddy had shot another smaller rat with a hand gun under the water heater in the kitchen. He was somewhat of a gun buff, so there was always some sort of loaded firearm nearby. The customer quickly disappeared, and I found myself in the kitchen with Daddy, rifle in hand—locked and loaded—stalking our prey.

Shortly we found him, nestled comfortably in a coil of extension cord between the refrigerator and the pie safe. Daddy was a crack shot, and in an instant, it was over. *"BAM!"*

I couldn't look. I knew the bullet had found its mark, and, being an animal lover, I hadn't really placed that wharf rat in the animal category until that moment. As Daddy gloated over his booty, I secretly grieved for Ol' Mighty. The bullet went clean through him and hit the wall, and as far as I know, is still there. Until we remodeled the kitchen years later, you could still see the slug lodged in the baseboard, marking Ol' Mighty's final resting place.

LIFE LESSON NUMBER TWENTY-THREE

Often, the "rats" in our lives leave the most lasting impressions.

CHAPTER TWENTY-FOUR

Franklin And The Dogs In The Pasture

My childhood experience was replete with "distant" relatives who occasionally came for visits, seemingly unannounced and out of nowhere. I'm sure it had been explained to Jean and me who those relatives were and where they were from, but as kids, we never remembered. All we knew was that, when they came, we were in for some *fun*!

One of our favorites was the family of Richard and Franklin, our cousins from somewhere way off; hence, they were "distant" relatives. Richard was closer to my age, and I really liked him. He was husky and good-looking, with blond hair and dancing, devilish eyes. Franklin was closer to Jean's age, and somewhat zanier than Richard. Yet, because of his advanced age (all of two or three years older than me), he seemed wiser and full of "street savvy."

This was proven one summer afternoon when Franklin came to visit. Since he was older, I was, of course, trying to impress him with my "playground," which was a huge (it seemed) pasture bordering our property. I think Richard and Franklin lived "in town" (Baton Rouge, Louisiana or somewhere like that), so they were always eager to come visit, as it gave them a chance to roam free, go fishing, and play unfettered.

Franklin and I had crossed over the fence and scrambled through the hedge row, and were headed out for "the hunt." I was armed with my trusty BB gun, hoping for some sort of prey I could shoot to further impress Franklin. What made me stop in my tracks, however, was not prey. In the clearing stood two of my (many) dogs, back to back, with their hind ends glued together! (In case you don't know—and I didn't at the time—this is how they make babies.) Suddenly I'm no longer trying to impress Franklin, but am now concerned for my dogs' welfare. After lifting my chin off my chest and catching my breath, I turn to the Wise One.

"What are they doing?" I screamed.

Incredulously, Franklin exhorts confidently, "They're ****ing!"

This, of course, didn't tell me a thing, as I had never heard that word before. "Well, get 'em loose," I shouted, which Franklin proceeded to try to do with the butt of my trusty BB gun.

The dogs eventually separated, but no thanks to the efforts of the Wise One. I did learn later the only person who can separate two amorous dogs in the throws of passion is Mother Nature. And I don't think I ever associated that litter of pups several weeks later with that traumatic day in the pasture.

LIFE LESSON NUMBER TWENTY-FOUR

People (and animals) are remembered for the "positions" they take in life.

CHAPTER TWENTY-FIVE

Butch's Addiction

I saw a sign recently at the local humane shelter advertising dogs for $75.00 and cats for $55.00. The prices are even higher at the pet store. I was amazed to think that what used to be free is now quite costly, particularly if you include "store bought" pet food and veterinary care. We didn't worry about shots and pet food in "my day." We just took our chances that our pet family wouldn't get sick, and left-overs and scraps from the table provided an ample (and "free") supply of doggy and kitty cuisine.

A major portion of my growing up years included managing a menagerie of various kinds of pets. Not only did I learn how to physically care for God's creatures, I also learned other valuable life lessons, some of which I didn't realize the impact until years later.

Take Butch, for example. He was from one of the litters born to the many mongrels that passed through my life. I had seen the movie, Ol' Yeller and read the book, Beautiful Joe, and early on, had developed a need to provide care and love for such defenseless animals. Butch started out as a cute, stocky little pup, and the only dog I ever had with a "curly tail." (I'd seen some of these in pictures and had always wanted one like that.) He was sort of the color of a palomino with a white collar and jet black eyes and nose. As he grew older, he was still small, but tough, and wouldn't take any crap off the other dogs in the neighborhood, regardless of size. His name (which I gave him) seemed to fit him perfectly, as he was constantly getting into "scraps" with any animal (not just dogs) that crossed him.

From Day One, Butch seemed to be fascinated with cars, and was immediately attracted to the "roar of the engines" around the corner from his little world in our back yard. If a dog can have a car-chasing addiction gene, I think little Butch had it. His car-chasing escapades would repeat themselves countless times daily, and if I was around, I would "spank" him mercilessly. After all, I thought, it worked when Mother did it to me, so why not with Butch? Surely, he'll learn his lesson.

But he never did. In fact, if anything, he only got worse. The more I spanked him, the more he chased cars. I firmly believe that my (innocent) abuse of him may have contributed to his antisocial ways and eventually his biting a little girl in the neighborhood. We were told that Butch had to be quarantined for ten days, because he might have rabies, but I knew better. My brand of "discipline" was just not working. After Butch's "assault" on the little girl, I noticed that I was the only person he would have anything to do with. It was "ego-gratifying" for me that, while he would snarl and growl at everyone else, Butch was like my own child and was totally devoted to only me.

Then one day I came home and found my friend, Joe, struggling with Butch by the side of the road after he had chased one car too many. In his zeal chasing the car, he apparently had not seen the other one coming in the opposite direction. It hit him squarely in the side, causing unseen internal injuries. Even near death, he would let no one come near him, so Joe had to literally kick him out of the highway. Although Joe meant him no further harm, Butch didn't know that, and Joe added insult (and possibly more injury) to injury as he hurled him to "safety" with each kick.

We all thought Butch was a goner, and because he was such a maverick, not many people were upset about it. Since my family didn't believe in veterinarians (after all, he was just a dog, and a mean one at that), and we might need that money later for the real doctor if one of us got sick, I just put him in a cardboard box and hoped for the best.

For the next several weeks, I was Butch's doctor, only leaving his cardboard box bedside to go to school, and at night to get some sleep myself. Miraculously, Butch pulled through, and gradually was able to get up and creep around the back yard a few minutes a day. Eventually, his addiction kicked back in, and the open road began to call (or shall we say, the cars and trucks of the open road!), and Butch's car-chasing behavior returned with a vengeance. Sometimes you just have to accept your pets—and other loved ones—as they are and love them unconditionally. Ironically, Butch lived to be one of the oldest dogs I had, and even with his faults, he was only one of three that I remember fondly by name.

LIFE LESSON NUMBER TWENTY-FIVE

Sometimes you just have to accept those you love just the way they are.

Top:
*The author's birthplace
in rural Crenshaw
County, Alabama.
Inset shows the view
from "down the road,"
circa 1944. The roads
are still not paved.*

Right:
The author, circa 1948

The early Moody clan approximately two years before leaving the farm.
From left: Daddy Moody, Annie, Mother (holding the author), Daddy
(holding Jean), and Uncle Vernon.

The author and his sister,
Jean, at Uncle Raymond's
gravesite, 1945.

Mama Norman and Daddy Norman as we all remember them.

This is the house where we lived in Columbus, Georgia for a short time before moving back to Crenshaw County and settling at The Triangle. Daddy's cousin, Alice (Moody) and her husband, Troyce let us stay with them and were very kind to us. The "family" took care of each other back then.

*The author and Jean in our new cowboy and cowgirl outfits,
Christmas, 1950. Daddy had just wrecked the car.*

*Jean, Mother,
and the author,
with The Triangle's
gas pumps
in the background.*

*Mother and Daddy,
open for business
at The Triangle!*

*The view between the gas pumps from our front door.
Standard Oil products were called Crown and Crown Extra –
or "Regular" and "Ethyl."*

Above:
*Daddy, getting ready
to sell insurance. Behind
him is Jean's bicycle before
the "conversion."*

Left:
*Mother, on Easter
Sunday. The Triangle
never closed.*

Mother, weighing up some "book bacon" and link sausage at the Triangle.

Mother, doing what she did best in her beloved kitchen.

The author, in the back yard at The Triangle, with part of his menagerie, including "Butch," right, at the height of his "addiction."

Coke bottles in the willow tree! The author got about half-way up before James took this picture.

1950's "cowboy" movie star, Lash La Rue. This picture was "personally" autographed for the author during a publicity tour to the Luverne "Walk-In" theater.

Now officially part of the family, Aunt Faye and daughter, Nancy, with Uncle Vernon.

The author, with Jean, Aunt Nina, and cousin, Nancy.

The author and Brenda. The ride on the scooter came much later.

The author with cousin, Nancy, and friend.

*The author's
first friend, Jimmy,
who was
already living
behind The Triangle
when our family
moved there.*

*This is Jimmy's
sister, Mary Ann.*

*Beautiful
"Little Liz."
We had already
attended the
sixth grade
banquet when
this picture
was made.*

*The author's
friend, Marvin.
He was a little
sensitive about
his droopy
left eye.*

This is Billy right after he joined the Air Force. He was stationed in Cheyenne, Wyoming.

Our high school principal, Mr. Harlan, the man with the "P.A. system voice!"

The Triangle in its heyday. Daddy paid $300 to have this aerial photo made. The actual "triangle" is clearly evident.

Jean, cutting the grass with our first lawn mower.
It was electric, so we were always running over the cord!

Jean, checking the mail. Since we lived in the store, we
got our "business mail" and personal mail in the same
big mail box.

Jean, striking a sunny pose at The Triangle. There's a "Standard Oil Products" sign just over her left shoulder.

Cousin Nancy, and Jean on the hood of Daddy's new 1953 Buick!

*Jean and Nonie in Nonie's front yard. The cotton gin is
just out of the picture on the left.*

*The author, in one of his favorite "publicity shots."
The Triangle (store) is just behind the sign.*

"Back to the farm." Jean strikes a pose on an old stump used for shoeing mules at Uncle Willie and Aunt Rebie's house.

Brenda, left, and Nonie "cheesecaking" in front of the mule pen at Uncle Willie and Aunt Rebie's house.

The way it used to be: Daddy Moody plows a dusty field of cotton with a mule.

A young Uncle Vernon takes a ride. Mules are forever!

CHAPTER TWENTY-SIX

The Day My "Baby" Died

To some people, it might seem silly, but my pets were like my family, and when one of them died, it was an extremely emotional time for me. Although my mother didn't share the same love for animals as I (she "tolerated" them), she was very compassionate and understanding when a member of my "family" passed away. There would be crying and wailing, along with the typical period of mourning and sometimes a mock funeral and burial, depending on the "closeness" of the relative.

None of my pets were pedigreed. (I didn't even hear that word until years after most of my pets had departed this life.) But they were just as loved and cared for as if they were champions. In fact, the scruffier they were, the more I felt a need to adopt them into the family, and they never failed to "re-pay" me with their love and devotion as well.

My most traumatic experience and subsequent lesson in loss and grief with my animal family occurred when I was about seven or eight years old. I observed many deaths over the years—in fact, too many to even list—but none were as significant as the tragedy of "Boots."

We didn't have Doppler radar and sophisticated weather-predicting technology in those days, and often, storms would find us ill-prepared for their suddenness. One late spring day, there came a particularly violent thunderstorm—a "frog strangler," as we called it. Spring in the South often spawns such weather, but on that day, the rain came down in sheets, and the thunder and lightning were nothing short of horrendous. I had always had somewhat of a fascination for storms, and would often enjoy just watching the fury from the back door of our kitchen at The Triangle.

But there was something different on this day. Over the din of thunder and pounding rain, I heard a faint but familiar sound. Having had many pets in the short time we'd been at The Triangle, I knew the sound of an animal in distress. There was a kitten out there! And it was in trouble! As the storm grew more furious, the poor kitten's cries became louder and more plaintive. *"Meow. . .meow. . .meow!"* Pacing the floor for several agonizing minutes, I would momentarily stop to peer into the rain-soaked back yard for any sign of origin of the pitiful wails.

Finally, I decided I'd had enough. Flinging the screen door open, I plunged into the stormy abyss. I could hear my mother scream as I raced aimlessly around the soggy yard. "Mike, get back in here! What are you doing?" In my zeal and haste, I almost stepped on the tiny creature. She was hardly as big as a grownup's thumb, and I was amazed that something that small could make such a noise! The kitten had obviously just been born, probably, I guessed, dropped by her mother on her way to deliver in a much safer (and drier) spot. Apparently "Mom" had been caught off guard by the storm's onslaught, and hadn't had time to make it to shelter before Boots made her grand entrance into my world.

I scooped the baby up with both hands and rushed inside, only to be met by my mother's skepticism. "Oh, Mike, why didn't you just leave it? It would've died anyway. Its eyes aren't even open."

"No," I sputtered, "She'll be fine….I'll take care of her….I'll feed her….She needs to be dried off….Jean's got a doll bottle….I'll get her some milk…"

Before I could finish stating my heroic plans, Mother had already handed me a towel. She knew that, when it came to animals, there was no need in arguing with me. I was going to take care of this kitten and do everything I could to save its life.

"You'll need a box to put it in," Mother said, "and you know you'll have to take care of it, or it'll die." She headed for the store to retrieve the box that would become Boots' home for the next several weeks.

Although Mother didn't allow animals in the house (growing

up on a farm, she was taught that), she occasionally made an exception for me—as long as they didn't "mess up the house," or as long as I cleaned up the mess. The goal, of course, was to get them out of the house as soon as possible. So, for the next two months or so, my life was devoted to Boots. (I named her that because she was solid black except for four perfect little "boots.") When she cried at night, I got up and gave her a bottle. When she flopped over on her back or was uncomfortable, I turned her over. When she wanted just to be held, I was there. I *was* Boots' savior.

As spring turned to summer, Boots began to outgrow her cardboard home (she'd already started to climb out), and we all decided it was time for her to go outside. Understandably, at first, she was apprehensive, but eventually she was scurrying around with the "big boys," and quickly adapted to life on the outside.

My mother had an incredible "green thumb," and passed some of her love for plants, flowers, and trees on to me. The morning was perfect when I stepped outside, and was greeted by the sweet smell of honeysuckle and other flowers Mother had lovingly planted in her garden. I had decided that my "project" for the morning was to get rid of some weeds around an apple tree she had set out a couple of years earlier. I had seen her weed the garden many times, so I thought I'd help her out today. So with gardening tools in hand, I proceeded to dig. As usual, Boots wanted to help, but I was on a mission. By now, she had become quite independent, and I shooed her away, eagerly anticipating the project at hand.

I was almost finished with the job, when suddenly I realized Boots was no longer pestering me. Partly out of curiosity, and partly out of concern for her safety, I momentarily paused from my labors to survey the yard. My weeding project was on the north side of The Triangle and near the front of the store, so I was always aware of the danger of cars and trucks, especially for my smaller pets. The sound of the car's engine starting instinctively drew my attention, but I was not prepared for what I saw next. There, under the rear fender of that car, was Boots, frozen in fear. The scream stuck in my throat, as the wheel quietly rolled over her limp body. Miraculously, she was still alive as I rushed to pick her up.

The rest of the day was a blur for me and my family. Everyone knew how devoted I was to Boots, and although they rallied around to lend support, no one had much hope for her survival. But somehow she made it through the day, and for several more weeks she clung to life. As the days grew into weeks, however, hopes for her recovery dimmed. Boots drifted in and out of consciousness, and although we all took shifts tending to her day and night, it was obvious she was suffering.

Then one day, Mother asked me if I was ready to let Boots go. I knew I wasn't, but I also knew I didn't want to see her suffer anymore. My friend, Byron, had offered to "put her out of her misery" with Daddy's rifle, and after a long and tearful goodbye, I let Boots go. We buried her near the spot I had found her on that stormy spring afternoon.

Years before the public debate over "mercy killings," I had already experienced the agony of putting my own feelings and needs aside in favor of mercy for another living being. Although I firmly believe in the sanctity of human life, I certainly understand both sides of this issue. And as tragic as Boots' story was, the experience undoubtedly prepared me for later inevitable and more significant deaths in my life.

LIFE LESSON NUMBER TWENTY-SIX

Grief and loss are a part of life; accept this lesson and live life more fully.

CHAPTER TWENTY-SEVEN

Roscoe Takes A Ride

I enjoyed watching the life cycle of the animals I had as pets, particularly the chickens. One of my favorites was a little white bantam (or "banty," as we called it) rooster named Roscoe I had raised from an egg. Roscoe was a cocky (no pun intended) little devil and, although small, he was like a drunk Napoleon in a country bar on Saturday night when it came to his "territory." He'd puff up and take on any size animal (or human) if he thought they were invading his space. Yet, he was a likeable little fella too, especially if he thought food was involved. He'd strut and crow, and engage in all kinds of tricks to get your attention. I even trained him to fly up onto my outstretched arm and eat corn out of my hand. Sometimes, in his zeal to find the tasty kernels, he would travel up my arm, perch on my shoulder, and actually peck at my teeth! I thought this was great fun, and delighted in showing him off to family and friends.

That is, until one day when my mother was hanging out clothes (right in the middle of Roscoe's domain). This was before we had a clothes dryer, so the clothes line was a necessary part of our back yard. Unfortunately, Roscoe mistook Mother's arm as his call to dinner, and blasted off toward the perch. All Mother saw out of the corner of her eye was a flash of white and the flurry of wings. She immediately and instinctively hunkered down, drawing her arms in to her side. This, of course, eliminated Roscoe's dinner table, and he shifted into overdrive.

If you've ever tried to reverse a banty rooster in upward flight, it's virtually impossible. So, Roscoe headed for the next highest perch, which was the top of Mother's head. Her screams brought my sister and me to the back door to see what was going on. It looked (and sounded) like an Indian war dance. Here was my mother dancing around the back yard, her shoulders even with her ears, pirouetting with the clothes still clutched in her arms, and poor Roscoe hanging on to Mother's hair for dear life. "Get this chicken off my head!" she screamed. Fortunately, I had a stash of corn in a nearby shed, and, grabbing a handful, lured Roscoe off his precarious perch and onto my arm for a fast getaway.

From then on, when Mother hung out clothes, she made sure Roscoe was locked up or had plenty of grub on the ground before sticking her arm out.

LIFE LESSON NUMBER TWENTY-SEVEN

Don't be "chicken" when you're trying to get your needs met.

CHAPTER TWENTY-EIGHT

The Trip To Gunter's Farm

There's an old saying down home that goes, "You can take the boy out of the country, but you can't take the country out of the boy." Having moved off the farm at age three, I still had a lot of "country" in me even years later, and often found ways to take a little of the country back to The Triangle with me. While the "city kids" had maybe one or two dogs or cats, I had a menagerie of all kinds of animals—rabbits, dogs, cats, chickens, turtles, goldfish—the list goes on. Most of those pets weren't acquired at a pet store (did they have those back then?), but rather were given to me by friends or relatives, or, in the case of my dogs, were thrown out by the side of the road near The Triangle.

I was particularly proud of my rabbits. The first one I had was, of course, named Peter, and was given to me when I was around six or seven years old. Some friends of my parents happened to have a female, and wanted to raise a brood, so they asked me if their female could "visit" young Peter. This was way before I knew anything about the birds and the bees (despite Franklin's attempt to "educate" me with the dogs in the pasture), so I figured, why not? Rabbits come into heat about every third day, so after a romantic week of love-making, Peter's girl friend was whisked away by her owners with a thank you to Peter and me for our hospitality.

"When she has babies, we'll bring you the pick of the litter," they promised.

Her name was Lucy, and she came to live with Peter several weeks later. And that's how I got into the rabbit business. Over the next two or three years, I somehow managed to put together enough cages to house, at one point, a maximum of 29 of the furry critters! In fact, I became quite well known for my "herd."

One of the people who took notice was the local Boy Scout Leader, Gunter Tamlin. I had been approached several times by friends who were already Scouts to join so we could all learn to tie knots in ropes and go camping together. Well, being a country boy already, I didn't really see any need in joining, because I already knew how to tie knots, and the great outdoors was already my playground. Besides, I was sort of a Mama's Boy, and didn't want to admit that I would feel a little uneasy spending the night in the woods without my mother around.

And then there was that nagging rumor that ol' Gunter was as "queer as a three dollar bill." I didn't really put much credence in it, because the boys usually laughed and joked about it, and besides, I wasn't going to join anyway. I'm sure my parents hadn't heard the rumor, or if they had, didn't believe it either. So when ol' Gunter showed up at the The Triangle to check my famous brood of bunnies and suggested I might want to see his, along with the other animals on his farm, nobody thought anything about it.

It was about nine or ten o'clock on a Saturday morning when Gunter and I headed out to his place about four or five miles down the Brantley Highway. It was already humid and steamy when we turned off the main highway onto the dirt road that led to his dilapidated old barn. It was eerily quiet, and, looking around, I realized we were far away from civilization as I had known it thirty minutes earlier. Gunter stepped out of the car, and motioned for me to come over to the wooden fence that extended out from the barn. I noticed there was only one horse—a mare—in the small pen and, since I wasn't much of a "horse person," I hoped he wasn't going to try to get me to ride her.

He appeared to be on a mission as he slid the bolt over on the gate and stepped inside the pen. I still thought nothing amiss as he disappeared inside the barn and emerged a few minutes later with a larger, much more spirited horse, which even I knew was obviously a stallion. Gunter joined me on the outside, and as "boy met girl," it still never occurred to me that he had more in mind than just breeding horses. After several minutes, the show was over, along with Gunter's excited remarks about the horses' private parts described in particularly graphic street terms.

I had always been taught to give a person the benefit of the doubt, and as my father put it, "If you can't say anything nice about somebody, don't say anything at all." However, by this time, I'm beginning to wonder about ol' Gunter, as I start to have flashbacks about my Scouting friends' seemingly unimportant warnings about his sexual orientation. (I learned later that homosexuality and pedophilia are two entirely different things.)

After the horse pen incident, it was as though the audio portion of my "camcorder" went on the blink, because I don't remember any conversation that followed, as the scene seemingly went into slow motion. *Inside Gunter's car. . . .Gunter reaching for the glove compartment. . . .magazines with pictures of naked women. . . .Gunter's hot, smelly breath and evil grin. . . .my protestations. . . .his laughter.*

Although he never touched me, the fear that he would was so overwhelming, I could scarcely choke out the words, "You. . .you know, my mother is gonna be wo. . .wondering where I am. . .she. . . she's probably got lunch ready by now."

Needless to say, I never joined the Boy Scouts, and over the years have wondered how many other boys had visited ol Gunter's farm and hadn't been as fortunate as me. As with most other victims of sexual abuse or attempted sexual abuse, it was decades before I told anyone of the incident. Remembering my father's admonition, I never told my parents what happened that day.

LIFE LESSON NUMBER TWENTY-EIGHT

Beware of wolves if you're in sheepish clothing.

CHAPTER TWENTY-NINE

Jim Bob's Handkerchief

I suppose every small town has at least one kind of weird individual that kids like to make up stories about. Sort of like Boo Radley in the Harper Lee novel, To Kill A Mockingbird, or Carl Childers from the movie, Slingblade.

Well, our town was no different. We had Jim Bob Walker. Although Jim Bob was harmless, he was a little scary if you didn't know who he was. He was a slow-moving, roly-poly, middle-aged man with short, thin, sandy hair. I never saw him smile, and his perpetually dour countenance made him all the more mysterious. Nobody knew too much about him (none of the kids, anyway). He'd just "show up" in town from time to time. None of us knew how he got there, but he'd hang around for hours, engaging in idle, nonsensical conversation with anybody who would stop and listen to him. The only thing I remember Jim Bob talking about consistently was his *gar-deen* (guardian), a family who apparently was responsible for his care.

Jim Bob was totally unpretentious, and, on hot summer days, would sweat profusely. His poor hygiene was particularly evident, as he would stand on the street corner and fan flies and gnats away from his face with his ever-present handkerchief. And when he wasn't using his hanky for fanning, he would turn it into a traffic flag, signaling that he needed a ride somewhere. Jim Bob wasn't hard to please, and would go in whatever direction the vehicle that stopped and picked him up was headed.

Everyone just sort of accepted Jim Bob as part of our small town culture, and nobody made a big deal about him and his strange ways. As the years passed, we saw less and less of Jim Bob and his handkerchief, and, although nobody talked about what happened to him, we feared the worse. We figured he died or his *gar-deens* died, and, with them, the end of an era. An era when less fortunate people could walk the streets of a small town without being mugged, taunted, or harassed. An era when *anyone* could hitch a ride *anywhere* and still find his way home at the end of the day.

LIFE LESSON NUMBER TWENTY-NINE

It's not so much where you're going; it's how you get there. In other words, it's the journey, stupid!

CHAPTER THIRTY

Porky Hits The Road

Before the days (and nights) of TV, VCR's, and DVD players, there was storytelling by grandparents and other "old folks." One of my favorites was a story my Aunt Nina used to tell me about an old woman and her pig. The gist of the story was that the old woman had bought a pig, but it was too big for her to pick up and carry, so she had to figure out a way to get the pig out of its sty and "drive" it home.

The story became long and drawn out, and with each attempt by the woman to get help to get her pig out, came more frustration. It started out with the woman asking a dog to bite the pig to get the pig to jump over the sty. It went something like this: "Dog, dog, bite pig. Pig won't jump over the sty, and I shan't get home tonight." Of course, the dog refused, and the woman would progress through the story until finally she found a butcher who would help her, and the story ended thus: "The butcher began to kill the ox; the ox began to drink the water; the water began to quench the fire; the fire began to burn the stick; the stick began to beat the dog; the dog began to bite the pig; the pig began to jump over the sty, and the old lady got home that night." Although Aunt Nina probably told that story to me hundreds of times, I never got tired of hearing it.

I was reminded of that story years later when I had to do a "project" for FFA (Future Farmers of America). I wasn't planning on being a farmer, but I was sort of forced into taking "agriculture" in high school and joining the FFA, because it was the only course I could take that year besides geometry. Our geometry teacher, Mr. Duke, had failed all but one or two in his class the year before, and I didn't want to run the risk of failing it too. (Incidentally, he was fired the next year for "failing" too many students. Go figure.)

So, I chose as my project, with the help of my Uncle Vernon, raising a pig from birth to market size (about 600 pounds). I was told I had to do all the feeding, tending, record-keeping, and weight-watching myself, which meant I had to have little "Porky" come and live with us at The Triangle. Baby pigs are rather cute and quite rambunctious shortly after birth, but quickly become a challenge to take care of as they grow older. I had to keep in mind that little Porky was not a pet, but a project for school, and eventually had to build a pen (or sty) out in the back yard for him.

Having left the farm years before, my parents were not into spending a lot of money on pig sties, so I set about finding materials already on hand to build it myself. There was always something old and wooden lying around, so before long, I had fashioned quite a sty out of some old 2 X 4's and 1 X 12's. I even found an old metal pan from the store to use as a trough to put the slop in. Hogs will eat literally anything organic, and in those days, you could feed them kitchen swill or whatever, and fatten them right up. They were natural, virtual garbage disposers!

Everything went well for several weeks, until little Porky started to grow (which was the idea, right?). Initially, he couldn't even see over the 1 X 12's that enclosed him. But now, he's not only beginning to *see* the outside world thanks to his fast-growing legs, he's beginning to get impatient with the food service—not to mention his boredom at being cooped up. With each feeding, his rudeness grows, and now when he hears the back door slam, he throws his front feet over the top of the enclosure, and nearly flops out before I can load up his dinner plate.

It was inevitable that little Porky (by now, *big* Porky) would discover that with a little more thrust from his hind quarters, he could scale the prison wall and be free to search for his own food. Pigs have this uncanny snout which they use to "root" or dig for morsels of buried food. That's how we first realized Porky had escaped. The back yard looked like a land mine had been stepped on, and Porky was nowhere in sight. Then the phone rang. It was one of the neighbor ladies on the line.

"Ain't Mike got a hog he's tryin' to raise up? Well, I think it's got out, and it's over here rootin' up my yard!"

And thus began the first of many expeditions to track down Ol' Porky and bring him to justice. News quickly spread about his daring escapes and subsequent romps through the neighborhood. The scenario was repeated almost daily.

Someone would report, "Mike's hog's got out again. There he goes!" I would then have to chase him down and herd him back to his pen, each time with increasing respect for the old lady in Aunt Nina's story. More often than not, it was my mother who would chase Ol' Porky down, because she was the only one available, with Daddy off selling insurance, and Jean and me off at school. Mother gained quite a reputation as a hog chaser before we finally got around to raising the walls on Ol' Porky's abode.

Eventually Porky neared the 600 pound mark and had to be exported back to Uncle Vernon's farm, much to the relief of our neighbors. I lost track of Big Porky after that, and didn't want to think about his inevitable fate. However, I did make an "A" on the project, thanks in part to Mother's hog-chasing abilities.

LIFE LESSON NUMBER THIRTY

If you ever decide to go "hog wild," don't do it in your own neighborhood.

CHAPTER THIRTY-ONE

Don't Mess With "Miss Lillie"

Don't get me wrong. "Miss Lillie" wasn't just some low-class country bumpkin who chased pigs, disciplined incorrigible children, and reprimanded ungrateful employees. She was, above all else, a nearly perfect mother. Her life centered around protecting and caring for her children. And, in my mind, she was the original "Stand By Your Man" woman, totally and unconditionally devoted to her husband. There was nothing she wouldn't do—and didn't do—to promote her family's well-being. She was, truly, the wind beneath our wings. Although she was a high school drop-out, she became the world's best cook, a nurse—and doctor, a psychologist, a gardener, a janitor and a maid, a Sunday School teacher (but not a preacher), and a business woman, just to name a few.

Mother was famous for her "fried pies," ambrosia, and red velvet cakes, plus many other dishes that she lovingly prepared for family and friends. One of my teachers in elementary school encouraged us children to thank our mothers for the meals they cooked for us. (Back then, a lot of mothers stayed home and did all the cooking.) I had never thought about it before, and had sort of taken her culinary skills for granted. After that "speech" by our teacher, however, I never ate one of my mother's meals without telling her how good it was, and how much I appreciated it.

I wasn't much of a breakfast eater growing up, and Mother was constantly trying to think of ways to trick me into eating breakfast. One day, she just came right out and asked, "Mike, what could I fix you for breakfast that you would eat?"

I thought for a minute and answered, "Well, Mother, you know

I really like fried chicken..." You guessed it. The next morning, I awoke to the sweet smell of fresh country fried chicken for breakfast!

I wanted to have the recipes for some of the delicious meals we enjoyed growing up, so years later, I had the presence of mind to ask Mother to write down some of her personal favorites. I knew that, if I didn't do this, future generations might never know the true joy of my mother's "southern home cookin'." Unfortunately, most were impossible to write down for "re-use," because it took her own personal touch to get them to turn out right. A few brave souls might want to try, however, so at the end of this chapter, I have included some of those recipes exactly as she wrote them. We tried for years to get her to open a restaurant, but she never even considered it, stating that she enjoyed cooking too much to ever make a business out of it. She'd rather just cook for the pleasure of it, and share it with family, friends, and customers. And that's exactly what she did.

In her "medical practice," Mother had an assortment of home remedies she used regularly with my sister and me. These included castor oil, camphor ice, paregoric, Ex-Lax, Feenament, and the dreaded hot water bottle enema. If there was one thing we learned the importance of, early on, it was "regularity." Our bowels had to move regularly (meaning daily), or measures were taken immediately to help out Mother Nature. We were usually given a choice of laxatives—the convenient chewable Feenamint or the tasty, chocolaty Ex-Lax. And woe be unto us if we didn't "go" by the next morning!

Mother was also a counselor/psychologist, and unconditional positive regard was her technique. She believed you "catch more flies with honey than with vinegar," so she was long on praise and short on criticism. Many nights we would have what Daddy called "settin' ups" to discuss problems that only Mother could help us with. The term "settin' up" (aka "wake" by the more affluent) was a reference to the practice of staying up all night when someone in the family had died. The theory was that the bereaved would have difficulty sleeping, so friends and relatives would "set up" (i.e., sit up as opposed to going to bed) all night and comfort and talk to them to help pass the time.

Although she had never had any formal training in horticulture (almost *all* of her training was informal), Mother was well known for her beautiful "flower gardens" on the grounds of The Triangle. It still amazes me that she could do all that she did—take care of two children and all the household chores, including cooking three full meals a day, managing a store, being "chief cook and bottle washer"—and still have time to create and tend to a virtual botanical garden on our little estate. I don't remember her ever using "store bought" fertilizer, but her plants were always the envy of the neighborhood. I guess you can't take the country out of the girl either!

There was one very important lesson Mother (and my father) taught me that, to this day, seems almost innate, and that is the principle of fiscal responsibility. Her philosophy was, simply, if you want something and you agree to buy it, you also make arrangements to pay for it. And she believed that the Golden Rule should always apply. With no training whatsoever in business or finance, she set about, shortly after we moved to The Triangle, learning the grocery business from the ground up. The Triangle was not a thriving business, so it was decided early on that we would offer something the big grocery stores didn't offer: credit. Although most of our "charge customers" were honest, hard working people who truly intended to pay their bills, many of them would "charge" at The Triangle, and then go downtown to the supermarket and pay cash, leaving us with their unpaid debts. Probably tens of thousands of dollars were owed to us over the years, and yet we had no recourse but to absorb them when people couldn't pay.

We were expected to pay our store bills weekly, however, and most of the wholesalers we purchased from understood our dilemma, and would sometimes "let us slide"—but not for long. Normally we would order our stock one day, have it delivered the next, and then pay for it the following week. We had one particular wholesaler which was owned by home town folks, so we preferred to do business with them, figuring they would be more understanding of our situation.

When my maternal grandmother, Mama Norman, got sick with cancer, and Mother was taking care of her at home, we got behind in our bills—not way behind, but enough so that it caused some concern for this particular wholesaler. Instead of calling and discussing it with my mother, the salesman came one day and took our order—much needed at the time—but never delivered the stock. The next day, Mother called the company and was told that they were sorry, but they couldn't deliver the goods because we were behind in our bill. Mother thanked them and told them that they need not worry, she would pay the bill. She often told us, "You can give out, but you can't give up."

Although we eventually recovered from that slump, and the bill was paid in full, Mother politely refused to do business with that company for the next 35 years, despite the efforts of countless salesmen. Her answer was always the same week after week, year after year. "No thank you; we don't need anything today." What she meant was, "We don't need anything from *you*." You just don't kick a friend when she's down. The Golden Rule rules!

Mother applied this rule to our customers as well. She was a very compassionate and giving person, and if you asked her, she would give you the shirt off her back. Or, if you had a problem paying your bill, all you had to do was talk to the "credit manager," and Miss Lillie would let you work out payments, all the while still letting you buy groceries on credit if you needed to. Once in a blue moon, somebody would violate her trust, though, and she'd write them off. She'd take their cash, but no more credit.

Sometimes we would get really upset about all the money people owed us and go on bill collecting sprees. After we turned 16 and got our driver's license, Daddy would even offer Jean and me a "percentage" if we could go out and get somebody to pay their bill. Mother showed us how this was done one day when we were coming home from the dentist's office. For a while, we made regular trips to a nearby town to go to the dentist because our teeth had fallen prey to neglect. Our one local dentist at the time knew how to do only one thing, and that was *pull* teeth, not *fix* them. His favorite expression was, "Come out, ol' toofy." And it would. Since I had acquired an awful sweet tooth from sneaking and eating candy right off the shelf at The Triangle, my "ol' toofies" had developed a lot of cavities. So we decided to go to our neighboring city of Greenville, about 20 miles away, and pick up a new dentist.

On our way back from one of those trips, we were about seven or eight miles from home, when suddenly Mother ordered my sister to pull the car over. Jean had been driving for about a year, and thought she had done something wrong.

"Why?" Jean asked.

"Just pull over right here," Mother answered.

And with that, she jumped out of the car and onto the front porch of the house we'd stopped in front of, and pounded on the door. Apparently there was no answer, and Jean and I watched in stunned disbelief as Mother grabbed a rocking chair off the porch and sprinted for the car.

"Open the trunk!" she hollered.

"Mother, what are you doing?" Jean asked incredulously.

Slamming the trunk, she explained, "These people owe me some money, so I'm just taking this chair in payment. Let's go!"

What the...? Our mother had just "stolen" a chair off some redneck's porch, and all I could think was, *Good Lord, we're gonna get shot!* Jean hit the gas, and we sped away, tires squealing, as Mother dusted her hands off in a triumphant gesture.

I don't know if those people ever knew what happened to that chair, or if they ever came back into the store. Other members of the family tell similar stories of Mother's daring heroics at protecting her interest in the store. All I know is, I saw a side of my mother that day that told me, if you buy something from Miss Lillie, you'd better pay up, or she'll come after you!

Another entire book could be written about my mother, so I won't attempt to encapsulate her in a few paragraphs here. I wrote and recorded a tribute to her endearing qualities, and presented it to her on Mother's Day in 1986. She was very appreciative of it, but being the humble person she was, shared it with only a few people. When she passed away in 1992, it was played in her honor at a very emotional memorial service. I felt obliged to include it in this book.

MIKE MOODY

MY MOTHER

My mother. . .what can I say about her that hasn't already been said about mothers since time immemorial? It's been said thousands of times by many much more adept with words than I. And yet, there's just still something special about my mother that begs expression, but defies description. Is it her compassion? For certainly she taught me the true meaning of the word. Like her concern for others less fortunate than herself. Or, for those whose families have been stricken with illness or death. The food she prepared. . .or the flowers sent. . .or simply the phone call with just the right words of comfort at just the right time. Is it her desire to do that which is right, even though it may not be the most popular or expedient course? I learned that at an early age. Is it her belief in the old-fashioned work ethic, even though an honest day's pay didn't always follow the honest day's work she did?

When I think of my mother, the old saying, "A man may work from sun til sun, but a woman's work is never done," takes on a whole new significance. While others may work themselves to death, my mother would die without it. Or, is it her courage in the face of seemingly insurmountable problems and adversity? Where did her strength come from when all others would have said long before, "Let's give up?" She'll give God the credit for that. Is it her beauty, despite her advancing years? Certainly, it's her inner beauty that endears her to all of us. Is it her IQ? You know, it always bothered her that she never finished high school. More likely, it's her "CSQ"—her common sense quotient—that has seen us through many a trial and tribulation. Maybe it's her perseverance—some call it "stick-to-it-iveness." That's the quality that made it possible for her to keep trying when the batter wasn't quite right for the biscuits, and the same quality that's kept the Mom and Pop grocery store I grew up with going for nearly forty years.

Can you believe, through all that, she still found time to nurse the sick, go fishing, work in a factory, take one vacation, feed, clothe and love a husband, two children and four grandchildren, teach Sunday School, and perform scores of other menial, yet necessary tasks, and emerge unscathed, and still going strong?

But, wait. We were searching for that something that makes my mother special. Maybe that's the problem. It's not just one thing. Oh, yes, it's all those other things and much more that make my mother special. Oh, we never said she was perfect; she'd be the first to admit that, and yet, it's her example that make us all want to strive for it.

MULES IN THE FAST LANE

So. . .here I am. Still trying to describe her. It can't be done, of course. So. . .I'll leave it for now, with the only words that, although worn from extended use throughout the ages, seem somehow to never get old. I love you, Mother.

MULES IN THE FAST LANE

Old Fashion Fried Chicken

1 or more chicken cut up
Salt & pepper to taste
Moist good with water or sweet milk
Flour good on all sides of chicken
Have frying pan about ½ full of oil
I use my old Iron Skillet and peanut oil
Let it get hot—put in chicken cook
slow turning as it browns on all
sides—about 35 or 40 min
depending on size of chicken.
Take up on paper towel to absorb
the oil and keep from being soggy—

Sweet Potato Casserole

About 6 nice sweet potatoes peel
and cook until tender—Drain off
all water and mash good
Mix 1 small can Pet Milk
1 cup sugar
1 stick Oleo
1 tsp Vanilla Flavoring
Mix until creamy—put in baking
dish that can cook in oven—

Topping
1 cup brown sugar (packed good)
1 cup flour
1 cup chopped pecans
1 stick Oleo—melt Oleo, mix
sugar and flour. Add pecans
last and mix on top of potatoes
and bake at 300 for 25 or 30
min, until golden brown

Ambrosia

*Use 12 or 14 oranges according to
size peel oranges, using each
section peel off all skin and
remove all seed.
Use 2 pks fresh frozen grated
Coconut—one cup or more
sugar to suit taste, takes more
for some oranges. Stir good—
Best to set & chill for awhile.
(Can use 2 small can crushed
pineapple if you like)*

MULES IN THE FAST LANE

Corn

Fresh frozen corn
put in heavy boiler & thaw good
Mix enough water to be thick
Add salt & pepper to taste
about ½ stick Oleo. Cook
until thick—then I cook in
oven for 30 or 40 min
until brown, but not dry—

                  for Can Corn

Season the same way and
cook in oven slow at 300
for about 30 min

MULES IN THE FAST LANE

Black eye peas

If frozen cook 1 hour or longer
I use scraps of meat to season
Can use strips of bacon or
scraps of ham and salt to taste
takes a lot of water sometime
they cook down fast—
If Can Peas, cook for 25
or 30 min and season the
same as for frozen.

MULES IN THE FAST LANE

Hocake corn bread

1 cup medium corn meal
1 tsp salt
enough water to mix good will
be soft
Cook in heavy skillet well greased
best to sprinkle a little dry
meal in bottom of skillet with
oil to keep from sticking. Cook
slow on both sides—Sometimes
might have to turn the second
time to brown good.
I double this & make 2 hocakes

Chocolate Delight

1—Mix 1 stick Oleo—(melted)
1 cup self rising flour
1 cup chopped pecans
Mix all this & press with hands
in 9 X 10 or 13 in baking pan
Bake at 350 for 20 min or until brown
Let cool—
2—Mix together 1—8 oz cream cheese
1 cup powdered sugar (10X)
1 cup C oil whip, put this
on top of the above—
3—1 small box instant chocolate
pudding mix—2 cup cold
S. milk—Mix good and
pour over 2nd layer—Chill
good before serving—

Quick Fudge

Mix 1 cup Pet milk
2 cup sugar
½ cup cocoa or 1 ½ cups
chocolate chip
½ stick Oleo—
Cook this for 5 min—
Stirring good & cooking slow—
Add 16 med. Marshmallows
(chopped) Cook this until melted
good—about 8 min—Beat
good and add ½ cup or 1 cup pecans
Put in buttered dish cool &
then cut in squares.

LIFE LESSON NUMBER THIRTY-ONE

Honor Thy Mother. . .

CHAPTER THIRTY-TWO

Daddy Keeps Things Interesting

Daddy had his own way of collecting money that was a little more confrontational than Mother's. He saw John D. Hollister in the store one day after he had failed to pay his bill as agreed. John D. was a "colored boy" who worked on the Pepsi Cola truck helping the driver haul drinks in and out of the stores. It was hard work, and you could generally tell somebody that worked on the "drink trucks," because, after several months of lifting those heavy returnable bottles, their muscles would start to bulge. John D. was no exception. He was short, but had been working on the Pepsi truck for a good while, and looked like a little Joe Louis.

But that didn't matter to Daddy. He caught John D. behind the vegetable cooler that day stacking some drink cases, and as John D. turned his hand truck around to leave, Daddy demanded, "John D., where's my money?" I don't believe anybody else was in the store at the time, and you could've heard a pin drop.

"Uh…uh, I'm own pay you Sad-dy, Mr. John," he stammered. (It was only, like, Tuesday.)

"No, you not, John D. You gonna pay me *now*, or you not leavin' this store." Daddy stood in his way, and for a few tense moments, it was a classic Southern style standoff.

Finally, his driver, Mr. Woodrow Martin, came to John D.'s rescue. (Besides, he couldn't leave him there; he needed him on the truck.) Woodrow's wife, Clara, had another little store on the other side of town, so we knew the family pretty well.

"'At's awright, John, let 'im go. I'll make sure he pays you."

Reluctantly, Daddy stepped aside, and John D. scurried out to the truck. John D. did pay his bill that Saturday, and I don't think he ever charged anything again.

Like my mother, though, Daddy believed in treating people fairly, and would come to our customers' defense if he thought anybody was trying to take advantage of them. There was an old colored man named Charlie Sims who was a regular customer at The Triangle, and always came in around the first of the month after he got his "check," and paid cash for everything he bought. Problem was, Ol' Charlie must've had what we now call gastroesophageal reflux disease, because he would eat the antacid, Tums, like candy. He erroneously called them "Tongues," because he couldn't read or write. When we say him coming, we'd almost crack up, because his request was always the same.

"Miss Lillie, you gots a box 'a Tongues?" Mother did eventually start ordering them by the carton, so he wouldn't have to come in every day or so, and could just stock up on them.

But Ol' Charlie had another problem. Because he couldn't read or write, he couldn't tell a one dollar bill from a twenty dollar bill. He would often catch a ride downtown to "the quarters" (the segregated Negro section of town), and, invariably, somebody would try to con him out of his money. Every time he'd come in to The Triangle, Daddy would warn him, "Now, Charlie, don't you go down there and let those people take your money." Then Daddy would proceed to try and show him the difference between one's, five's, ten's, and twenty's. I don't think he ever did learn, though, and you could always tell when he'd been ripped off, because he'd run out of money before the end of the month.

Always the sagacious businessman, after he stopped drinking and quit his insurance route, Daddy developed a keen sense for bartering and trading. He started what most people now call a pawn business, and could "turn a buck" sometimes in a matter of minutes.

One day, after I grew up and left home, I had come home for a visit, and Daddy abruptly announced, "Come on, let's go to town a minute." Since he rarely asked me to go anywhere with him, I was curious, so I agreed. It was only about two miles to town, and as we turned off the main highway, I recognized the road as an area where one of Daddy's cousins, Max Washington, lived.

Max must have been expecting us, because he met us at the door. He was a small man of few words, so with a brief, "Hey, how ya' doin'," he motioned for us to follow him. We entered his bedroom, and on the bed lay a shotgun, and hunting vest and two boxes of shells. I still didn't know what all this was all about, so I kept quiet as Daddy picked up the gun. He softly stroked it, turning it over and inspecting it as a jeweler would inspect a fine diamond.

"What'll you gimme for it?" Max asked. Then it dawned on me why we were there. Daddy didn't need a shotgun, but he knew he could re-sell it and he must've known Max needed the money.

"Give you $50 for it," he muttered.

"Aw'ight, then," Max answered, "you can have the vest and the shells too."

The transaction took less than two minutes, and we were on our way back to the store, where Daddy propped the shotgun up in a corner behind the cash register. Later that day (probably an hour or so), a customer came in to the store and saw the shotgun in the corner.

"Hey, John, whatcha want for that shotgun," he asked.

"Oh, I'll take three hundred for it," Daddy said. Apparently, he had already anticipated the question and was ready with the price.

It was partly deals like that which allowed my father to accumulate a comfortable nest egg, pay off all his bills, and leave this world debt-free, quite a feat for a man who—although he eventually quit drinking—had been a hopeless alcoholic for over 30 years.

Daddy also had a penchant for musical instruments and gadgets. One of my first memories of him was seeing him try to play the guitar. He never really mastered it that I remember, but incredibly, he could play the harmonica by ear, and occasionally he would get the old "mouth organ" out and amaze us all by playing whatever tune we could name.

When it came to gadgets, he was always the first in town to get a new one—whatever it was. For example, he bought a reel-to-reel tape recorder (a Truetone from Sears) before most of his friends even knew what it was. He also got one of the first CB radios in town, and was a charter member of the Good Sam CB Radio Club after getting the craze going in the community. A favorite activity for Daddy was to record customers without their knowledge when they came into the store. He would then play the recording back for them, and after they got over the initial embarrassment, everybody would get a big chuckle out of it. For a time there, you had to be careful what you said, because you never knew if you were being recorded.

Not only did Daddy like *having* gadgets, he liked *inventing* them too. One of his most ingenious ones was an item that, unfortunately, he didn't get a patent for, and which eventually became a very well known and popular staple in most cars. It was the infamous cup holder.

When he was still selling insurance, none of the cars he drove had air conditioning, so on hot summer days, he would often stop and pick up his favorite (non-alcoholic) beverage—Coca Cola. He got tired of trying to hold on to the bottle while driving, and had no place to put it when he made frequent stops to collect insurance premiums. So, one day he went to the local awning/carport company and got one of the workers there to fashion a cylinder of aluminum that had a hanger he could conveniently attach to the inside of the car door. It was "custom designed" to hold the six-ounce returnable bottle, and Daddy used it for many years.

In addition to his practical side, Daddy also had what I called his "rascal" side. He had a great sense of humor, and was quite the joker at times. When manufacturers first put turn signals on cars, he bought a 1951 Chevrolet and told me that these new cars were so smart, they knew when and where you wanted to make a turn. He said they would activate a "blinker" that would point in the direction the driver intended to go. To prove it, he took me for a ride, and, sure enough, as soon as he said he wanted to turn onto a certain street or road, that blinker mysteriously started blinking! It was months before I realized that he was sneakily turning it on himself.

Daddy liked excitement too. If it wasn't happening, he *made* it happen. He loved holidays like the 4th of July and New Year's because it gave him an opportunity to shoot off fireworks and engage in other roguish activities. His favorite was wrapping up several sticks of dynamite and shooting at them with a rifle. He tricked me into shooting the bundle one New Year's Eve by telling me that the shooter couldn't really hear it or feel it like other people, and somehow explained it away scientifically. I fell for it, and, after a couple of cracks with the rifle and missing the target, I hit it the third time dead center. Daddy was right about one thing. The shooter *didn't* feel it like everybody else. It was worse! The force of the blast felt as though my eyelids curled up over my eyebrows, and I couldn't hear *anything* for the next several days.

Only his "inner circle" of friends and relatives knew Daddy was doing it, and, although he did it regularly for years, it always created an uproar in the community. Although Mother didn't get the kick out of it Daddy did, she usually went along with it just because she knew he enjoyed it so much. Following the explosion, unsuspecting (i.e., non "inner circle") neighbors would call us and ask, "Did y'all hear that? It shook my windows," or "It knocked my dishes off the shelf!" Mother would always play dumb, and eventually it would blow over—until the next big holiday.

It didn't have to be a holiday, though, for Daddy to cause a stink about *something*. There was this one cantankerous old couple who lived sort of behind The Triangle. They were quite stodgy, and the man's wife was always complaining about something. One day she called us and told us that the smoke from our trash pile was blowing over into their yard. We didn't have garbage pick up in those days, and everybody had their own trash pile where they burned their trash. And it was just kind of understood that smoke "came with the territory."

Well, apparently this complaint didn't set too well with Daddy, because it took him only about ten seconds after hanging up the phone to go out and throw a couple of old tires on the smoldering heap. The lady should have quit while she was ahead! That fire burned for about two days with the blackest, stinkiest smoke the neighborhood had ever seen. I don't remember her ever complaining about anything we did again.

As with my mother, an entire book could be written about my father's escapades. It was no secret that he had some bad habits that neither he nor his family was proud of. But, as most people do, he eventually "straightened up," and made us very proud to say he was our "Daddy." One of his greatest accomplishments was to conquer his alcohol addiction. He joined Alcoholics Anonymous, and became a devoted "Twelve Stepper," remaining sober the last 17 years of his life, and helping countless others achieve and maintain a life of sobriety one day at a time.

As I did for my mother, I wrote and recorded a tribute to my father and presented it to him on Father's Day in 1986 also. Here is a transcript of that recording:

DEAR DAD

Dear Dad. You know, that says it all. Somehow it seems harder to talk about our dads; we're supposed to be tough, you see, and not show our feelings, but somehow, right now, it seems appropriate to turn that around and let me tell you about my Dad and how I feel about him.

By the way, it used to be "Daddy" back when I was "Bambino," as he called me and, really, in a way, he's still "Daddy." He'll always be that, even though us grown-ups have changed it to "Dad," and he'll always be dear to me. So. . .Dear Dad does say it all, but, you know, the funny thing is, I don't think I've ever really told him. . .not out loud, anyway. In fact, there's a lot of things I've never told him. So. . .I guess now's as good a time as any to "settle up" and set the record straight.

Where do I start, though? That's the problem. Maybe I could start with a few thank-you's. Like for those late-night "settin'-ups," as he called it; those times when we had to stay up just a little later than normal to work out our problems. They seem so small now to have seemed so big back then. Maybe I could thank him for the times he was up late thumbing through that big insurance book, getting ready for work the next day while I was sound asleep. He did that for twenty-three years, you know; he said it was so I could have all those things he never had.

Now that I have children of my own, I can appreciate the sacrifices he made for me. While I'm at it, I'll thank him for all the times he did manage to come home early enough for me to have the car for that special date. Or, maybe for the time he slipped me that hundred dollar bill when I thought I wanted to get married. And then, of course, for those times when we couldn't get him to go home to the store keeping he loved because he loved my mother more, and wanted to stay with her when she was in the hospital.

Hey, let's face it. There's just not enough time for all the thanks that are due my Dad. Oh, there were some bad times, too. Everyone knows that, and, he'll be the first to admit it, but, you know, the memory of those times grows dimmer by the day, as I remember the good times we shared. Like when he tried to fix breakfast when Mother went to work at the "sewing factory," as we called it. Or, like the "Good Egg" pin Brother Walker gave him for going back to church regular. Or, the time he chased the "bad guy" down who crashed into the front of our living room and then tried to drive away.

And, although Daddy never professed perfection, he never had to teach me how to be a man. He simply showed me. He taught me important things, too, though, like, "If you can't say anything nice about somebody, don't say anything." That's been one of the hardest for me to swallow. And, things like. . .it's O.K. for a man to cry when he's hurt. One of the most important things he showed me is how a Daddy can love his child and let him know it without even saying it.

Well, I don't know if I'm as good at that as he is, but there is one thing I do know how to do, even though, through the years, I've done it very little. And. . .just in case I forget to do it in the years to come, I'll do it now, and hope he remembers it. And that is to say these four words, and mean it with all my heart. Daddy. . .I love you.

LIFE LESSON NUMBER THIRTY-TWO

Honor Thy Father. . .

CHAPTER THIRTY-THREE

Daddy Chases The Bad Guy

Maybe it's just me, but it seemed that my childhood was full of excitement—not just the normal good kind, like going to "The Fair" and riding the roller coaster, but sometimes just plain weird, unbelievable, exciting stuff.

One such occurrence happened one night at suppertime. Believe it or not, there was a time when we (and other families) actually sat down at the supper table at night and enjoyed a nice meal and fellowship together. However, this particular night proved to be anything but idyllic. What seemed to be an ordinary meal with my mother, father, and sister was suddenly shattered by what sounded like an explosion. The whole house shook, and, instinctively, the four of us were on our feet and out the front door to see what had caused such a commotion.

Somehow we knew something had happened "out front," as that's where the "parking lot" for The Triangle was, and naturally where all the action usually took place. Although it didn't take but a few seconds to vacate the building, I'm sure we were all conjecturing: *explosion, a wreck, an earthquake, the rapture?* Well, not exactly. Upon exiting the front door, we discovered the source of the disturbance. To our right was a scene from a movie which Hollywood couldn't have staged any better. There sat a 1949 Ford, its rear wheels perched on the three-foot wide curb that extended across the front of the store, and the back of the car buried in the outer wall of our living room! Apparently the drunk at the wheel had misjudged the distance when he thrust his car in reverse (or maybe he thought it was in "drive") and, flying backwards, had jumped the eight-inch high curb and deposited his rear end squarely under the double windows of our living room.

The original structure was all wood, and quite old, but this part of the building was fairly new, as it had been added onto the store a few years earlier to provide our living quarters. Although the windows and inner wall remained intact, the outer wall was no match for the drunken man's battering ram. We didn't know whether to laugh or cry, and, needless to say, we were all incredulous as we approached the smoky debacle of shattered wood and crushed metal, and the man rolled his window down. Other than Daddy's expected cursing, ranting, and raving, I don't remember his exact salutation to the drunk man. However, I do remember vividly the man's response as he turned to his female companion.

"I guess I better pull up and see what kinda damage we did...or what kinda damage *I* did, rather."

As the man eased the car into drive, it slowly inched forward, and we held our breaths as the rear wheels slammed onto the pavement. Then, *zap*, in an instant the car was gone, speeding north on Highway 331!

Daddy was somewhat of an "ambulance chaser," and liked nothing better than being in the middle of the action. In fact, he was probably the first person in town to get a police scanner so as not to miss a single action-packed minute of the adventures of the Luverne Police Department or the Crenshaw County Sheriff's Office.

I heard Daddy bark to Mother, "Call the police! I'm goin' after 'em!" as he sped away in a spray of gravel and dust.

Call it fear, disbelief, Post Traumatic Stress Disorder, or whatever, but I have no recollection of anything after that until Daddy drove back into the yard, stepped out and began relating his story to Luverne's Finest. Apparently Daddy had chased the mavericks quite a ways up Highway 331 until they finally careened off onto a dirt road. At this point, Barney Fife Moody managed to find a wide enough spot in the road to pull alongside and fire three shots into the galloping Ford from one of his trusty sidearms. (He always carried a German Lugar and a 9 mm something or other in the glove compartment.)

Well, as expected, this put a stop to the chase and to my father's temporary insanity of single handedly bringing these criminals to justice. Both cars screeched to a halt, and for what I'm sure seemed like hours but was more like a couple of minutes, it was a Mexican Standoff. As his car's headlights illuminated the back of that '49 Ford, Daddy finally began to think rationally. *What if I shot the man? What if he's going to come back here and shoot me? Why don't I get the H*** out of here?* As reason, for the first time that night, took over, Daddy slowly backed away and drove back to The Triangle.

The story goes that, about two weeks later, the '49 Ford was found—less its previous drunken occupants—abandoned in the little community of Rutledge, about six or seven miles from where Daddy gave up the chase, with three bullet holes in the trunk. The driver and his companion were reportedly never found nor identified.

The only reminder of that bizarre night is the gaping hole under our living room window, which remains to this day, covered only by the aluminum siding we installed several weeks after the incident.

LIFE LESSON NUMBER THIRTY-THREE

There's a reason we have police; take the law into your own hands at your own risk.

CHAPTER THIRTY-FOUR

I Didn't Know Blood Had Lumps In It

As you can see, my father had his own unique way of taking matters into his own hands. As an adult, I have talked to many people who relate various life experiences to me that can be described, at best, only as dull. In fact, one of my best friends in school was once referred to years later by his wife as "…just your good ol' garden variety vanilla," meaning that, even as an adult, his life had been fairly uneventful. He even told me once that he had never been depressed and never had a headache!

Well, I have been and had both, but they paid for some incredibly fun and exciting times. I always knew that even though things looked bad (or "dull"), if I just waited long enough, *something* would happen to stir things up!

Daddy was the kind of guy who wanted to know everything that was going on. I think he got that from his mother, because she was always asking incessant questions. One day, after quite a lengthy and tiring (for me) interrogation, I asked my grandmother, "Annie, why do you ask so many questions?" Her answer was simple. "Well, it's the only way I can find out what's going on!"

Because Daddy was so "inquisitive," he never missed a chance to find out about anything and everything that was happening in our little community. Even before police scanners and CB radios, Daddy had an uncanny ability to get right in the middle of "police business." One night he heard that somebody way out in the country had gotten shot or stabbed or something. So, naturally, we got in the car and drove out there. When we drove up into the yard, we noticed a few other "brave souls" were already there. (I wondered if they were family, friends, or just curiosity seekers like us.)

It was an unusually dark night, and as I followed Daddy up the steps of the old unpainted, dilapidated, clapboard house, illuminated only by the police car lights, I was taken aback by the sight on the front porch. The police cruiser had a single red light on top (standard in those days) which gave a periodic eerie glow as it flashed across the scene. Apparently the victim had fallen prey at, or near the front door, spilling blood clear to the front porch steps. Sidestepping the carnage, we walked into the house, which obviously had no electricity. It was thick with stale, smelly air, and black as pitch. It was only my father's hand that kept me from falling into Hell, as I thought surely this must be what that place is like.

Since we couldn't see much, we weren't inside very long. Exiting the building, Daddy let go of my hand, leaving me alone on the porch. Reflecting back, I am still amazed that I didn't get sick because, as I looked down and my eyes adjusted to the darkness, I saw what looked like clumps of *something* floating in the bloody mess. As I stared downward, wide-eyed, I wasn't thinking, *Why am I here?* or *Isn't it strange that my daddy has brought me way out to the middle of nowhere in the middle of the night like this?* My only thought at that time was, *Gee, I didn't know blood had lumps in it.*

What may have seemed to some like a weird and unusual night was merely chalked up as a normal "ambulance chase" for Daddy, and a chance for me to pick up some of my grandmother's penchant for questioning *what's going on?* Incredibly, however, that night and its bizarre events were never mentioned again by me or my father, and, even though I know better, I still wonder from time to time if blood really does have "lumps" in it.

LIFE LESSON NUMBER THIRTY-FOUR

Sometimes it's fun to be scared, but sometimes it's scary having fun.

CHAPTER THIRTY-FIVE

"Judy" Sets The House On Fire

Even before there were Barbie dolls (at least in south Alabama), there were little plastic dolls with frilly dresses, silky hair, and eyes that closed when you laid them down. I don't know how many other girls had them, but over the years my sister, Jean, had amassed quite a collection. Since this style of doll was not the kind you would drag around and play with "full time," our mother thought it would be nice to display part of Jean's collection in a handy corner shelf she had strategically placed on the wall, coincidentally, over the space heater in our bedroom.

We didn't have central heat (and no air-conditioning!) in those days, but felt we had "arrived" when we got natural gas and those individual gas space heaters in each room. I'm not sure whether the heater was placed in the corner first, and then the shelf, or vice versa. Nevertheless, there they were, on that cold winter day, sharing the corner of the bedroom Jean and I shared.

I believe it was late on a Saturday morning, because Daddy was still home. (He usually worked his insurance route in the afternoon.) Suddenly in what seemed like a flash, the house and store were filled with thick, gray, stinky smoke. We literally couldn't see our hands in front of our faces, but fortunately, were able to stumble our way outside. Daddy stayed behind to call the fire department which responded quickly. Since we lived only about two miles out of town of around 2,500 people (which was considered "out in the country" then), it didn't take long for them to come to our rescue. I'll never forget our chagrin when the firemen stormed the house, axes and hoses drawn, and shortly thereafter emerged with Judy (I'm not really sure of the doll's name, but Jean had named them all), charred to a crisp after unexpectedly falling off her shelf onto the blazing heater. Even before the days of invasive government regulation, heaters back then had "protective" bars in front, purportedly to keep ignorant heater owners like us from accidentally burning ourselves. I guess the manufacturer hadn't anticipated little "Judy" flying off her lofty perch and landing precisely in the middle of the flaming inferno.

Fortunately, there was no other damage except from the smoke. Daddy was a heavy cigarette smoker, and he joked about how he wasn't the only one smoking that day! It took us a week to blow all the soot out of our noses.

LIFE LESSON NUMBER THIRTY-FIVE

Don't smoke in the house; something might catch fire.

CHAPTER THIRTY-SIX

The World Is On Fire

It didn't have to be such things as firemen coming into our house to keep things interesting around The Triangle. It seemed that there was *always* something to do. Sometimes it involved work, and sometimes it involved play; it just depended on how you looked at it. In addition to all kinds of people parading in and out of our living room to buy groceries or whatever, it should also be noted that we lived just far enough out in the country for us kids to continually "explore new horizons."

One of those horizons was our back yard and "points beyond." Although fairly small, it seemed quite large at the time. It was full of interesting "things"—animals to play with, fences and trees to climb, especially in the nearby pasture, and all manner of "junk" lying around to build things with—just to name a few.

In our little Mom and Pop store, my sister and I had ready access to the "candy counter." Over time, though, Mother had to teach us discipline when we would visit that tasty spot in the store; otherwise we would have eaten up all the profit! Even so, as a result of that particular "perk," Jean and I didn't have any trouble making friends, because Mother would usually let us treat them when they came over.

Two of those friends we used to "treat" regularly were Shirley Ann and Pauline. Their family had moved into a house not too far down the road from The Triangle, and soon we got to know them pretty well. Shirley Ann was about Jean's age, and Pauline was just a little younger than me. Pauline was sort of a tomboy, so we hit it off immediately and became fast friends.

One crisp, cold, *dry, windy* winter day, the girls made the trek from their house to The Triangle. As usual, after the visit to the candy counter, we all started looking for "something to do." Shirley Ann and Jean quickly departed to play their own "little girl games," leaving Pauline and me to fend for ourselves. It would seem strange today, but back then, we thought nothing of "playing with matches" because we were taught early on to "take out the trash" and burn it in the corner of the back yard. It didn't seem at all unusual, and, even as children, Jean and I had performed the ritual many times.

Pauline was intrigued with the idea of burning something, and, being eager to impress her, I suggested we "go to work." The problem was that, on that particular day, we had no trash to burn. No problem, I assured her, we'll find something else to burn. I raced inside for a box of "Strike Anywhere" matches (they're more impressive if you're trying to "show off"), and, in a flash, we were huddled over a small pile of straw near the trash pile.

"We're workin', ain't we? They're playin', but we're workin', ain't we?" I rhetorically and confidently asked Pauline, referring to Jean and Shirley Ann.

Apparently we couldn't have special ordered better conditions for a prairie fire because, before Pauline could answer, *whoosh*, the world was on fire! If I hadn't known better, I would have thought Shirley Ann and Jean had poured gasoline on the back yard!

Although Pauline and I made it to the back door before the conflagration overtook us, I might as well have stayed out there, because my tail got *burned up* later by my mother!

The fire department said there was really no danger to the house and store, but Mother had to set new standards for the use of matches and trash burning after that.

LIFE LESSON NUMBER THIRTY-SIX

If you're trying to impress a girl, say it with flowers. . .or anything but matches!

CHAPTER THIRTY-SEVEN

Billy Buys Me A Pipe

Having grown up in our little Mom and Pop store, I was exposed to the sale of, not only your standard variety of groceries, but also many other well-known retail products. We called our store The Triangle Service Station and Grocery, and, although it was relatively small, we carried an amazing assortment of items to fill almost any want or need.

We had a "notions" section that included everything but snake oil. (We probably had that too; we just didn't call it that!) Some of the brand names were Hadacol, Carter's Little Liver Pills, and Lydia E. Pinkham's Vegetable Compound. Jokes would frequently surface about the wild advertising claims of many of these products. For example: "Did ya' hear about the guy who took so many Carter's Little Liver Pills, that, when he died, they had to beat his liver to death with a stick?" (The name was later changed to Carter's Little Pills when it was determined that the "medicine" didn't actually do anything for your liver.) The claims for Hadacol became so preposterous that we heard stories about amputees growing arms and legs after taking it. This probably had to do with the fact that the main ingredient was alcohol! When Ray Stevens came out with his 1961 hit, Jeremiah Peabody's Poly Unsaturated Quick Dissolving Fast Acting Pleasant Tasting Green and Purple Pills, I often wondered if he had gotten the idea from our "notions" counter.

By the time I was four years old, I could tell you the name of every cigarette, snuff, or tobacco product on the market. My maternal grandmother dipped snuff (I think it was Tube Rose), and my father smoked two to three packs of cigarettes a day. I never had a desire to partake in the consumption of either of these products. In fact, I learned to hate cigarettes with a passion, as Daddy smoked constantly, and the putrid smell of cigarette smoke was ever present in the house and store. I did, however, become intrigued with pipe smoking. I must have seen someone smoking a pipe in a movie or in a magazine and thought it was "cool." I knew my mother didn't like cigarettes or cigars, but I'd never heard her say anything about pipes, so I somehow got the idea that maybe I could try one.

So, one day I decided I'd go on a mission to obtain my own personal pipe. Although we sold Prince Albert tobacco in the can, most of our customers used it to "roll their own" (cigarettes), and a pipe was considered a nuisance for them. Some of the "old-timers" could tap out a helping of Prince Albert onto an OCB cigarette paper, roll it up and lick it shut quicker than most others could get a ready made Pall Mall out of the pack. We had no market, then, for pipes, so I knew I'd have to somehow find one "downtown," maybe at someplace like the "Ten Cent Store."

Mother had hired a high school kid named Billy to help us in the store, and I thought he might be the answer to my problem. Certain kids were known to be smokers, and the local high school even had an unofficially designated tree where some of the students were allowed to go out and smoke under. I knew Billy was a smoker, so I started working on him to help me accomplish my mission.

Billy was a really cool guy. He had curly jet-black hair, and rugged good looks that made all the girls swoon. But he was also a down-to-earth kind of guy who took up a lot of time with my sister and me in between his duties at the store. He would even sometimes buy us stuff, and once bought me a BB gun, which he spent a whopping $5.00 for—at that time, about a week's part time salary for him.

I knew I couldn't just come right out and ask for a pipe, so I started dropping hints about going to town to "look around" at the Ten Cent Store. This didn't seem too unusual to Billy, because it had become a tradition for Jean and me to go to town on Saturday afternoon to buy a toy—sort of as a reward for good behavior during the week. Billy had his own car and, finally, after several days of "hints," he took me downtown just to "look."

I had been in the Ten Cent Store many times and knew my way around. I remembered seeing some corn cob pipes there on an earlier trip, but I wanted something "classier." I guess I was taking a little longer than Billy thought I should, so he started asking me what I was looking for.

"Well, I'm sorta looking for a…something like a…a pipe," I stammered.

"A pipe?" Billy asked. "What kind of pipe?"

"Well, you know…a…a pipe like you put in your mouth."

I began sweating as I made a motion as if placing a pipe into my mouth. Still hovering around the corn cob section, I could tell Billy was becoming leery as he steered me down another aisle.

"Here, this must be what you're looking for," he said as he reached into a small bin of knick knacks.

My heart sank, and I knew it was over when he showed me a tacky little plastic "bird" pipe which was popular with the younger kids. You could fill it with water, and blow into it, and make a chirping sound like a bird!

I was mortified that Billy would think I wanted such a worthless piece of junk. Nevertheless, I let him buy it for me, knowing that weeks of "conning" were going down the drain, and my quest—at least for now—to enter the exotic world of pipe smoking was over.

Fortunately, I was able to shake the obsession, and, to this day, have never smoked a pipe or used any other tobacco product, for that matter. Although he continued to smoke, I'm glad Billy, even at age 17, had enough common sense to steer me in the right direction.

LIFE LESSON NUMBER THIRTY-SEVEN

Smoking is for the birds.

CHAPTER THIRTY-EIGHT

Can Birds Really Talk?

Being a former "farm boy," I had an innate love for animals, and was always fascinated by the life cycle of cows, pigs, rabbits, turkeys, chickens, and guineas my grandparents raised on their farms. At some point, I had heard about a small parrot-like bird called a parakeet that could actually be taught to talk.

My sister and I had heard about a man who raised them to sell, so we started putting pressure on our parents to get us one. We'd seen our grandparents' chickens and turkeys reproduce, so we figured, if we played our cards right, we could get one for each of us—a boy and a girl—and maybe raise some of our own.

After much deliberating about whether we could properly take care of them, who would take us to get them, where the money would come from, and so on, it was settled. We promised we would become devoted bird watchers, and that we would do without lunch at school for the rest of our lives in order to pay for them. Fortunately, it didn't come to that, and our Uncle Doc agreed to, not only buy them for us, but to drive us to the aviary in Union Springs, a small town about an hour and a half away, to pick them up.

The place was in the middle of *nowhere*, and, after what seemed like hours of driving, we pulled up in front of the man's house. Doc had brought a $20.00 bill (a fortune in those days) to cover the cost of two birds at $6.00 each, and a cage for $6.00. We spent the rest on "supplies" and bird seed.

The birds were housed in a small "barn," and, when the four of us entered the building, we were immediately covered up with para-keets! The old man had obviously been fooling with the little birds for a while, because he could literally pick one out of the crowd (of hundreds?) and catch it with his bare hands. I chose a green one, and Jean picked out a blue one. It turned out I had gotten the male, so I named him "Pete." Jean called hers "Toots."

To say that our foray into the parakeet business was a disappointment would be an understatement. In spite of our efforts at matchmaking, the two little critters seemed to hate each other, and constantly fought and screamed at each other like an unmatched married couple. I saw only one egg during their "career," and I think they ate it for breakfast one morning.

Nevertheless, I was determined to find some redeeming quality in our feathered friends, and decided to make it my goal to teach little Pete to talk. I'd done some "research" and found out a few pointers that were supposed to make this happen.

First, I separated him from his irascible female companion. Then I isolated him in my room in a separate cage someone had "donated" to me (obviously from someone who had gone out of the parakeet business). I kept the cage covered, and spoke to him *only* the words I wanted him to repeat back to me—simple words like "hello" and "pretty bird." When this failed, I even ordered a record produced by a "professional bird linguist." Simply playing this record daily was guaranteed to teach even chickens to talk—or so the advertisement claimed.

I spent countless hours faithfully playing the record over and over to little Pete, but, other than a few chirps, peeps, and squawks, he never uttered a single intelligible word of English.

In spite of their failings, however, Pete and Toots became an important part of our family, and were eventually reunited to spend their remaining months as reluctant husband and wife. When they both died—just days apart—we commissioned our Uncle Vernon, who had taken a mail-order taxidermy course, to stuff them for posterity. Although he did the best he could, it wasn't a pretty sight, and eventually they were afforded a proper and fitting burial in their final resting place in the back yard.

LIFE LESSON NUMBER THIRTY-EIGHT

You can't teach an old dog new tricks. . .and you can't teach a bird English!

CHAPTER THIRTY-NINE

Back To The Farm

Although I have many memories of "experiences" growing up in a rural setting, some of my memories are simply of "things" that don't necessarily have stories behind them, but were, nonetheless, "rememberable."

Both my maternal and paternal grandparents were hard-working "country" people, squeezing a living by the sweat of their brows out of eighty acres of sandy, sand-spur infested farm land. Although most of my memories of time spent with them are warm, some of the nights spent there were bitterly cold. "Heaters" were, of course, unheard of, and what little heat there was came from a small fireplace in what we would now refer to as the "living room," aptly named because (if you didn't want to freeze to death!) that's where most of the living took place.

I don't think there was any such thing as insulation back then, especially at Uncle Willie and Aunt Rebie's house. Jean and I sometimes spent the night there too, and the house itself was an adventure. The heating system consisted of one fireplace and an old wood-burning stove (for heat *and* cooking). It was an ancient clapboard place that had never seen a drop of paint, and although they had indoor plumbing, indoor bathrooms were not part of the décor. It was reminiscent of Snuffy Smith's house in the Barney Google comic strip, and you could literally see the stars at night through the holes in the wooden shingled roof and hear the crickets and critters through the holes in the walls!

There was a well in the front yard which supplied all the water for the cooking, bathing, etc. The only thing that kept a person

from falling into the well was the 3' X 3' wooden housing which surrounded the hole and supported the pulley for the bucket. The water
had to be drawn (i.e., "cranked up") on a rope attached to the bucket.
A metal dipper was handily hung on a nail for quick drinks on hot
summer days. The water was always cold—summer and winter—and
better than Perrier!

Uncle Willie was sort of "laid back," and Aunt Rebie was always laughing, especially when she would let slip an occasional "cuss
word." Never at a loss for words, she is the only person I ever knew
who could talk while breathing out and in!

And then there was my cousin, Nancy, with whom I liked to
climb on top of my grandparents' outhouse and eat Oreo cookies. It
seems rather obscene to think about now, but it made perfect sense at
the time. The smelly little hut was nestled in a quiet, shady, isolated
corner of a pecan grove, making it ideal for blissful "reflection." We
enjoyed climbing on top because it was actually cleaner on the tin
roof than at ground level (and a lot less stinky!). Although it wasn't
that high, we thought you could see the world from up there. Plus, we
were inaccessible to dogs, hogs, and other varmints that would invari-
able try to steal our cache of cookies. It became somewhat of a ritual,
and we would sometimes spend hours snacking, talking, laughing,
and just enjoying the coolness of the shade on a hot summer day.

Nancy had a sister named Cynthia, who was born with an "en-
larged heart" and given very little chance of surviving. Her mother,
my Aunt Faye, was, even then, a true "steel magnolia." She literally
carried little Cynthia on her hip for ten years before her death. Cynthia never walked or talked, as she was also afflicted with Mongolism,
and was severely mentally and physically retarded. I always admired
Aunt Faye and Uncle Vernon for not "putting her away" in a home
somewhere, or having her institutionalized.

Aunt Faye was a lot like my mother. She just did what she had
to do. I never remember her complaining, even when she caught her
arm in the old "wringer washer" or when she had to get up way before
dawn and drive to the "boonies" to pick up "hands" to work on the
farm (and sometimes do the work herself).

One of the things I remember Aunt Faye having to do was to chase down ol' "Jerry" periodically and bring him back home. Jerry was a big bull Uncle Vernon had bought from a neighboring farmer. Problem was, Jerry had a little age on him and was kind of set in his ways. Apparently he never got to where he felt at home on Uncle Vernon's farm, and, when he got homesick, he'd just go back to Mr. Gafford's place. Forget fences, or roads, or ditches, or whatever. When ol' Jerry got it in his head it was time to go "home," nothing stopped him. Sometimes his former owners would try to scare him off with a few blasts from their shotgun, but to no avail. It became a regular occurrence to make the trek over to Mr. Gafford's, and drive or haul ol' Jerry back. Eventually, he got too old to roam, and finally "retired," but not before he put a lot of "miles" on all of us.

Mr. Gafford's farm and others in the area were all identified geographically as being near Finley Hill. Everybody knew where Finley Hill was because that's where the "fire tower" was (and still is). It was the highest "place" around, and, over the years, when local kids talked about it, it began to take on a personality of its own. We were *never* allowed to climb up the tower, so we just made up stories about it which became local folklore, especially with us kids.

"It's so big up there, they've got a whole living room suit up there," we'd say, or "You can walk around in that big room." In reality, there was *nothing* up there but a panoramic view of the surrounding forests and barely enough room for more than a couple of people to get in there. The mystique was, "It is so high up there, it looks real small, but it's actually *really big*." The rumors just got out of hand.

Memories of "back on the farm" abound, and are as varied as they are numerous. For example, when those "distant relatives" would come to visit, it was always a challenge to find a place to sleep. Grandma's feather bed (immortalized in John Denver's mid-seventies hit song) really did exist, and sometimes *would* hold eight kids, provided you squeezed 'em in sideways! Hotels and motels weren't that prevalent, and were never considered anyway because, well, you just didn't put "family" up in a motel. Pallets were popular means of providing respite and were sometimes nothing more than a blanket or quilt placed in an out-of-the-way corner.

Once, when cousin Barbara and her brood came for one of the holidays, Uncle Buddy—who was almost blind—came stumbling through one the bedrooms in the old farmhouse, not realizing that one of her babies had been bedded down on the floor. This particular pallet was more in the line of traffic than an out-of-the-way corner, and, apparently Uncle Buddy's boot grazed the baby's head and jarred him just enough to suddenly awaken him.

Stumble. . .stomp. . .stumble. . .stomp. "Wah!" Michael screamed.

"Ungh!" Buddy grunted.

"Oh, my God!" Barbara yelled. "Buddy stepped on the baby's head!"

In seconds, thirty people were in that room, all trying to scoop up little Michael, with poor ol' Buddy reeling from the invasion, and wondering what had just happened. Michael probably messed in his diapers, and must have thought it was Armageddon. Talk about a rude awakening!

Sometimes during those "get-togethers," we would look for ways to entertain ourselves, particularly at night. Daytime activities revolved around farm work (and play for the kids), but nights were time for relaxing and unwinding. Those nights we spent there were not shattered by the roar of oozies, bombs, and machine guns on TV (that didn't come along until years later), but rather in the cozy laps of our grandmother, Annie, or great aunt, Nina, as they told familiar stories of old, like Br'er Rabbit and Tarbaby in the briar patch, or the midnight ride of Paul Revere. Aunt Nina would make the sound of horses' hooves on an old hard cover book, and the effect was heart-stopping! I never tired of hearing her tell that story over and over. The Grand Ol' Opry on radio was popular also, and if the reception was bad (FM didn't come along until years later, either), we would crank up (literally) the Victrola, and play a few gospel or country songs, all under the watchful eye of General Douglas MacArthur, whose portrait was proudly displayed above the fireplace.

The house was always filled with good smells too, especially at mealtimes. The food just seemed to taste better when cooked on the old wood-burning stove, and there was nothing like home-made biscuits softened with butter we churned ourselves with milk we got right from ol' Bessie. Sometimes we'd sweeten up our biscuits by poking a hole in them with our finger and filling them with freshly made cane syrup. The main course would often include possum (and 'taters), rabbit, fried chicken, and homemade "tea cakes." Unfortunately, the "secret recipe" for those incredible tea cakes died with my grandparents; yet I can still taste them in my mind.

There were always interesting things to do outside in the country. Like exploring the corn crib, the hay barn, or the "potato house." The potato house was an intriguing place. It was a small shed-like building, the roof of which was about two feet from the ground. We thought it was air-conditioned, because it was sunken into the ground, and stayed cool and dark (to keep the harvested potatoes from sprouting). It had shelves around the top of the inside walls for storing canned foods, jellies and preserves, all made with fruits and vegetables from the farm.

My maternal grandfather, Daddy Norman, was a tall, husky, jovial man who was fond of playing dominoes with the neighboring farmers or relaxing in the front porch swing after a hard day of farm work. Not infrequently, the chain holding the swing would give way under his bulk, and send him crashing to the floor in a resounding clatter. He would normally sustain only an occasional bruise, and the news would quickly spread that Daddy Norman had fallen out of the swing again! He always took these spills good-naturedly and in stride, and we all thought it was great fun. When he wasn't relaxing, Daddy Norman was sometimes "manufacturing" hickory hammer handles, hoe handles, and shovel handles with a draw knife. His workshop was an old weather-beaten tree stump in the corner of the yard. I was amazed at how he could play a tune on a leaf simply by popping it into his mouth and "blowing." (It never worked when I tried it.) He was the world's loudest sneezer, and occasionally we could hear his "spasms" echoing off the hills as he plowed the fields with his old mule.

Both sets of grandparents lived "way out in the country," so when we went to visit, we had to make sure we took plenty of "supplies" with us. At our grandparents', we couldn't just jump in the car (there wasn't one, and I don't remember my grandparents ever driving), or step into the store like we could at The Triangle and get whatever we needed.

We did, however, have a phenomenon that brought the store to us out in the country. It was the "rolling store." The rolling store was a "panel truck" with shelves inside stocked with all sorts of goodies. The truck usually had a wooden dowel chicken coop tied to the front bumper. I once asked if they sold chickens, and was told that, to the contrary, the driver would sometimes take chickens (or eggs, or butter) in exchange for goods if his customers didn't have cash to pay him. Even though my sister and I always had all we wanted at The Triangle, it was quite a thrill to have the rolling store come rumbling down the road and stop by for some quick on-the-spot shopping. I bought a box of Milk Duds once that tasted like pepper. We talked about that for weeks and speculated about the weird taste. We figured the driver must have spilled some black pepper in his truck and hadn't cleaned it up very well!

None of the roads to my grandparents' houses were paved, and it was sometimes a challenge negotiating them, especially after a heavy rain. We were always admonished to "stay in the ruts" lest we "end up in the ditch." After the roads dried out, another phenomenon would emerge: the "road scraper." You could hear it coming if you were outside, and we would rush to the side of the road and eagerly await the big machine, puffing smoke and "scraping" the ruts out smooth until the next big rain.

Obviously, weather conditions were always uppermost in the minds of farmers, as it affected how their crops turned out. But my paternal grandmother, Annie, took it a step further in the winter. She must have been taught somewhere in her youth that it was imperative to wear hats or caps or bonnets when it was cold. Jean and I paid her no mind, though, because all we wanted to do was go out and play! Being the matriarch (and one of the original "steel magnolias"), it was her job to take care of *everybody*. And, since I was "the baby" (i.e., the youngest child in the family), Annie would usually "call the roll" before the warning about headgear.

"Aub…uh…John…uh…Vern…uh…Mike!" she would sputter. "Put sump'm on ya' head!"

When we would dart outside, we used to see how far away we could get before she finished that sentence!

I was really impressed with Annie. What an interesting grandmother! Although stricken with arthritis during the time Jean and I were visiting her back on the farm, she didn't let it stop her from being active. It used to literally take her thirty minutes or more to get out of bed in the mornings, so it did slow her down quite a bit, but once she "got going," she did whatever she had to do. She made no bones about her love for her family, especially her grandchildren. She often quoted one of her favorite poems, much to the delight of all of us. *"I love you little; I love you lots; my love for you would fill ten pots, twenty buckets, thirty cans, two washtubs, and three dishpans."*

One project I remember Annie taking on was raising turkeys. I'm not sure how she got the idea, but she already had a few of the big birds, which we, of course, enjoyed on holidays like Thanksgiving and Christmas. She knew that the life cycle took a little longer for turkeys than chickens, so she got the idea to collect turkey eggs and let her chickens set on the eggs and hatch them out. She wasn't sure it would work at first, but she knew that, once chickens are ready to "set," they'll do it on rocks or bottles or whatever!

So, over a period of several months, Annie hatched out hundreds of turkeys, which she shared with friends and family, and even started selling for some extra cash. The plan was so prolific that her son, Vernon, finally had to tell her to slow down. The turkeys were taking over the yard!

Before winter would "set in," there would be the harvest, consisting primarily of corn, peanuts, and cotton. And pecans, if you were fortunate enough to have some trees on your land. Uncle Vernon also grew sugar cane, and made his own cane syrup. He built the "mill" himself, with bricks he'd collected. At first, it was fired with hardwood, but later he "went modern," and installed a propane gas tank and burners, making it easier to regulate the heat. He squeezed the juice out of the cane with a contraption he made by connecting a long belt to his tractor. The juice would run down a trough into a long metal pan to be slowly cooked and poured off as the finished product—thick, dark, sweet, delicious cane syrup.

But it gets better. My grandmother, Annie and my Aunt Nina would take the syrup inside and cook it some more. If there were cooking thermometers, we must have not known about them. I guess the "old-timers" had done it so long, they could just tell, by looking, stirring, and feeling when the consistency was right. As the goo simmered at just the right temperature, it would thicken even more, and everyone would grab a hot glob. Before long, we were having ourselves an old-fashioned candy pullin'!

If all went well—temperature, consistency, and weather—the result was a golden yellow "taffy" we called, simply, syrup candy. Money couldn't buy a better tasting treat on a crisp fall afternoon.

Sometimes we would just let the syrup set and "age" in the jar or can for a period of weeks or months. And, again, if the conditions were right, the syrup would naturally crystallize into chunks of pure crystal-clear sugar. We called this treat "rock candy," and it was almost as delicious as syrup candy.

Corn was probably the least exciting of the crops, although it was a vital part of the curriculum. At its peak in the summer, it was a daily staple at meal time, usually cooked right on the cob, or scraped off and served, cream-style. Later, in the fall after it dried, the corn was shucked and stored in the corn crib, an old, generously "ventilated" wooden shed, equipped with its own hand-crank sheller. On almost any day, you could find Uncle Buddy out at the corn crib shelling corn for the chickens, and competing with scores of rats and mice for their next meal. Of course, the cows and hogs enjoyed their own "corn on the cob."

Peanuts were a little more fun. In the fall, they were pulled right off the vines and boiled in a salty brine for a delicious, nutritious treat. I guess I led a "sheltered life." I was in my 20's before I found out that this was almost exclusively a southern tradition. I'm amazed even today that there are still people who have never heard of boiled peanuts. On the other hand, almost everyone has heard of roasted peanuts; however, we always called them "parched" peanuts, an expression you still hear in some parts of the Deep South.

Peanuts had become very popular in our part of the country due to the devastating cotton boll weevil. Most of my generation remembers the expression, "When cotton was king." Cotton in the Old South was *the* crop of choice until the boll weevil came along and ate up all the profit. Farmers started looking for ways to recover from the little monster, and then really did start "working for peanuts." In fact, the little nut became such a savior that a small community in a nearby county erected a monument in the town square to the infamous boll weevil. It was their way of thanking the varmint for steering farmers in the region away from cotton and toward the peanut. My understanding is that this is the only monument to an insect anywhere in the world. Necessity is indeed the mother of invention (or, in this case, the peanut).

But still, by far, the most fun crop for us kids was cotton. The fascination with cotton for us was partly due to the fact that, by the time my sister and I came along, the more "well-to-do" kids didn't have to labor in the fields picking it, and could enjoy the perks of its harvest in many different ways. For example, Uncle Vernon would park his large cotton wagon in the corner of the yard after a hard day of picking by "hired hands," and let us kids dive into it and roll and frolic around in it to our heart's content. Problem was, once in a while, a stray boll with its hard shell would find its way to the surface and give us quite a stick with its sharp pointed end. I honestly believe this is where someone got the idea for the trampoline—diving into a wagon load of freshly picked cotton and jumping back out after landing on one of those prickly pods!

I still remember my mother and father telling stories about how they picked cotton all day long, dragging a burlap sack that would hold three hundred pounds when full. It would take six bags full to make a bale (1800 to 2000 pounds), and, if you were good, you could literally "pick a bale a day." To this day, I prefer cotton shirts to all other fabrics, and often wonder if anyone ever thinks about the colorful history of cotton, and the sacrifices our ancestors made just to get it out of the fields.

LIFE LESSON NUMBER THIRTY-NINE

You can take the boy out of the country, but you can't take the country out of the boy!

CHAPTER FORTY

Earl And The Runaway Mule

My sister and I have a lot of childhood memories of what we consider quite a unique upbringing. Sometimes we share those memories, and compare how the stories differ. She insists that she doesn't remember this one, even though it stands out for me as one of the funniest.

As far as our family was concerned, we didn't have an "official" place to go fishing, except what we called the "County Pond." We never went fishing there, though, for several reasons. For one, it cost money, and our philosophy was always, "Why pay for it when you can do it for free?" Besides, any place that collected water, eventually would have fish in it, and there we'd go! Another reason was that it was too far away—probably six or eight miles from The Triangle (seemed much farther back then). To this day, I have never been to the County Pond.

But one day, we did go fishing with our Uncle Doc. It was early summer, and the birds were singing, bees buzzing, and critters crawling. Somehow we had made it over to our grandparents' house, and Uncle Doc loaded us up in his old truck. (I don't think they made new trucks back then; they were all old, dirty, and broken down!) We got a fairly early start, and our "gear" consisted of three cane poles and some worms we had dug up out of the yard.

We set out down the one-lane dirt road that ran by our grandparents' house. I don't remember how far we went, but I do remember it was far enough to be shady, cool, and damp when we finally stopped the truck and got out. We still had to walk quite a ways to get to the fishing hole. Don't ask me where the "boat" came from, but there it was, all of a sudden. Even though I had never learned to swim, I felt safe with Uncle Doc. He had fought in the war, and we knew that, no matter what happened, Uncle Doc would take care of us.

I don't think we caught any fish that morning, but that didn't matter. We were having *fun* just being with Uncle Doc, and chilling out on a hot summer day. After what seemed like too short a time, Uncle Doc decided it was time to go, and we started back to the truck. It was quite a trek; so on the way back, we stopped for a few minutes to rest.

That's when we heard "noises" from around the bend. Soon the clip clop of hooves was followed by none other than little Earl Carnley, shouting orders to his insubordinate, runaway mule!

"Whoa! Stop! Come back here! Whoa!"

Uncle Doc was already starting to laugh as Jean and I looked at each other wide-eyed. I'm sure the old mule didn't plan it, but just as he got within spitting distance, he snorted and kicked up his back legs as if to say to Earl, "You ain't tellin' me what to do!" He then methodically "broke wind," letting out the loudest fart we had ever heard!

Poor little Earl was slightly older than Jean, and had had a "crush" on her for a long time. But from that day on, we never thought of Earl without remembering his old mule and how long it took us to stop laughing—long after he and his flatulent friend disappeared around the next bend!

LIFE LESSON NUMBER FORTY

Being "stubborn as a mule" can have more than one meaning.

CHAPTER FORTY-ONE

"Wawst" Nests, 'Lectric Fences, And Medicine

If my childhood was anything, it was certainly not boring. I've often wondered if I got more than my share of fun and excitement, and maybe that's why some kids didn't seem to have any!

As both my maternal and paternal grandparents were farmers, much of my childhood was spent visiting them on weekends and in the summer, as well as holidays throughout the year. There never seemed to be a lack of fun things to do on the farm, and I am still amazed today at the number of kids who tell me they are bored. There were always eggs to collect, corn to shuck and shell, animals to feed, and of course, fishing!

My paternal grandmother, Annie, had a nephew named Aubrey, who came to live with my grandparents when I was a youngster. Aubrey was probably the most colorful character of my childhood. My Uncle Vernon let him help on the farm for his "keep," and I remember how he liked nothing better than driving the tractor. He had swarthy skin and calloused hands from years of hard work. He had very few teeth, but that didn't stop him from "gumming" most anything he wanted to eat. He had a raspy, infectious laugh, and a penchant for telling the boys dirty jokes and reciting his favorite "nasty" limericks. He was "tough as nails" and rarely wore shoes, even in the dead of winter. With his bare feet, he would stamp out cigarette butts, step on "stickers" (briars and sandspurs), and walk on hot pavement, nails and broken glass without so much as a whimper.

But the most amazing thing about Aubrey was his uncanny ability to pull wasp nests down with his bare hands, apparently without incurring a single sting! Fishing was one of our favorite pastimes when visiting Annie and Daddy Moody, and Aubrey always delighted in securing our favorite fish bait, wasp larvae, from under the eve of a barn or outbuilding. While we would be screaming and running for cover, Aubrey would be calmly walking away with his treasure, adult wasps swarming angrily, and he, laughing heartily. It never ceased to amaze us kids, and we would ask him incredulously, "Aubrey, don't they sting you?" He always had a couple of standard answers, neither of which satisfied or convinced us. Slapping his hands alternately under each armpit, he would declare, "I just do this before I pull 'em down!" (We never really saw him do this, so this explanation didn't seem plausible.) His favorite explanation, which he confidently declared with a devilish grin, was, "Aw, yeh, but it don't bother a man!"

Although he was my cousin, Aubrey was much older, and, in fact, had children my age. We didn't have much to do with them, though, because apparently they "sided" with their mother when she and Aubrey separated and he came to live with my grandparents. He kind of "adopted" Jean and me, and affectionately referred to me as "Sugar Boy."

Uncle Vernon was very sharp and somewhat of an innovator as farmers go. He was always looking for ways to make the farm more efficient and productive. One of those innovations was the electric fence. Aubrey had sort of a devilish sense of humor, especially when it was at somebody else's expense, and it was he who introduced me to this modern day marvel.

It was on one of my many trips to the farm to visit my grandparents, and, as usual, Aubrey was tending to his various chores when we arrived.

"Hey, Sugar Boy, come here. I got a surprise for you!" He shuffled off toward the back yard with an expectant grin. At first, I didn't see anything, but then he pointed to the ground.

"See that right there?" he asked.

Well, it didn't look like much of surprise to me—just a wire about a foot off the ground strung around part of the back yard. It looked like he was trying to keep some hogs penned up with that little strand of wire. I thought, *this must be another one of Aubrey's jokes*, not realizing what an understatement that was.

"Yeh, what is it?" I asked.

"Just reach down there and grab hold of it with both hands," he snickered.

I didn't even know there was any such thing as an electric fence, but I found out later that this one had an alternating or pulsing current that went through it about every two to three seconds.

Suspecting Aubrey was up to no good, I replied, "Why?"

"Just grab it," he insisted.

Well, I figured, what harm can there be in a little piece of wire, so I slowly reached for it, not noticing the twinkle in Aubrey's eye getting brighter.

Apparently I grabbed the wire just as the current had passed through, so I felt nothing. I immediately let go of the wire and, looking up, asked confusedly, "Why did you want me to do that?"

Aubrey could hardly contain himself as he fired back, "Just grab hold of it and hold on!"

The last part of his command wasn't necessary because, as anyone knows who has ever grabbed a wire with 2,000 to 10,000 volts surging through it, you *can't* turn it loose!

The charge caused a spasm in my muscles, forcing my fingers to tighten around the wire in a death grip. As my eyes rolled back and my body convulsed, I felt my hair shoot straight out and my feet leave the ground!

That was probably the longest two or three seconds of my life, and, when I finally shook my hands free, Aubrey was already in tears with laughter, his bare feet dancing with glee.

He was eventually able to muster, "Are you O.K., Sugar Boy?"

"…Uh, well, I…I guess so. What *was* that?" I cried.

"That's a 'lectric fence," he said. "Don't ever touch it!"

His exhortation seemed a little late, but I guess it was his way of teaching a little boy the dangers of electricity.

I got Aubrey back one day, though, when we went on a mission to give some of Uncle Vernon's new pigs some screw worm medicine. We had stopped at the pasture, and Uncle Vernon, Aubrey, and I got out of the truck and crossed over the fence into where all the hogs were. The idea was to not cause too much of a scene, as the mother hog (or "sow") was quite territorial and protective of her brood. I don't know that Uncle Vernon or Aubrey had ever been "gored" by a sow (the older ones had some pretty sizable tusks—or "tushes" as we called them), but we didn't want to take the chance. We had to be sneaky and catch each little pig one at a time, pop some screw worm elixir into the little squealer, quickly turn it loose, and repeat the process until they were all medicated and before Mom knew what was going on.

We quietly got set up in the corner of the pasture, and Uncle Vernon grabbed his first "patient." The little porkers were kind of slippery, so we were glad to get hold of the little guy without too much difficulty. Suddenly Vernon made a startling discovery. He had forgotten to bring the medicine!

The way I saw it was, here we were, huddled down in the corner of the pasture with a kinetic handful of squealing dynamite, surrounded by a mother lode of suspicious sows, waiting to make us their next meal. No problem for Uncle Vernon, though. It wasn't too far back to the house, so he instructed Aubrey to just "hold on" while he drove back to get the medicine.

Now, Aubrey was a pretty tough character, but he didn't want to get into a fist fight with an 800 pound slab of bacon, so he called on me to protect him.

"Here, Sugar Boy, take this stick and keep that sow off of me!" And with that, he threw me a "stick" about a foot long, and hunkered down with his little porky pal. By this time, the little fella was squealing his lungs out, along with a few piggy karate kicks thrown in for good measure, and Mama Hog was bearing down on both of us with "tushes" bared!

I figured the best defense was a good offense, so, I courageously raised my weapon in a threatening gesture, and charged forward, screaming my fiercest war cry in the gruffest voice I could muster.

"G...g...get back! Get back!

Well, I might as well have been singing opera, because Mama Hog never broke her stride, and pretty soon my charge became a cowardly, backward, tap-dancing retreat. I could hear Aubrey's plaintive cry behind me.

"Don't let that sow get me! Hit 'er! *Hit 'er!*"

Just as I was about to backward step over Aubrey's head, I stopped cold, and, tiptoeing on my right foot, leaned forward in a precarious stance just far enough to tap the old sow on the tip of her gigantic snout.

Tap. *Roar!* Mama's battle cry shook the meager stick from my trembling hand, and I never looked back as I raced for the fence, clearing it in one magnificent leap.

When I finally did look back, I could barely see Aubrey at the far end of the pasture, as he had made a hastier and more distant retreat than I had.

Mama and baby were, of course, instantly reunited, much to our chagrin. Although I hadn't planned this little caper, I secretly remembered Aubrey's earlier shenanigans and wondered if he'd wished he'd had that electric fence to throw at that old sow!

You might say that, with Aubrey, "what you saw was what you got." We thought he was about the funniest guy around (when he wasn't playing dirty tricks on us kids!). Yet, he had his troubles too, which no one liked to acknowledge or talk about. His fondness for "the bottle" was no secret among the family or the townspeople. And we had all heard for some time that he had "fits," one of which I had the horror of witnessing in my back yard one day while showing him my menagerie of rabbits. It was an Aubrey I had never seen, and my first viewing of a full-blown epileptic seizure. It happened without warning, and even if I had been warned, I'm not sure I would have been prepared.

Aubrey was standing behind me, and I had just asked him a question. Getting no response, I turned around just in time to see him, glassy-eyed, open his mouth, drooling saliva and blood, and curl down into a huge fire ant bed! With heart pounding, I raced inside, screaming for help. Apparently Uncle Vernon had seen them before, and reassured me, "Oh, he's just having a fit." Nevertheless, Uncle Vernon still had to get him out of the fire ant bed, which he did by shoving him with his foot lest Aubrey grab him with flailing arms and drag him down too. In a few minutes, it was over, and nobody talked about it, but the scene was burned into my memory.

Sadly, Aubrey was killed years later when a similar seizure threw him off the tractor and under the Bush Hog it was pulling. We all took solace in the fact that he died happy—driving his beloved tractor.

LIFE LESSON NUMBER FORTY-ONE

Don't send a man to do a boy's job.

CHAPTER FORTY-TWO

Asleep At The Wheel

Although I didn't really have to do the grueling, back-breaking work it took to run a farm, I did enjoy being there when it was taking place. Most of my childhood was spent outdoors, and going to my grandparents' farms was an ideal way of getting out of the house (and to get out of working in the store).

Every season had its unique share of "chores," but I liked the summer most of all because the days were longer and, therefore, afforded the opportunity to be outside longer. Uncle Vernon was a hard worker, and I don't think he ever slept. When I would spend nights on his farm, he would already be up and "working" when I stumbled out of bed in the morning. And, late into the night when the "cobwebs filled my head," he would still be going strong.

There was one night, though, I did see Uncle Vernon go to sleep. It was at the end of a long, hot summer day, and I had been tagging along with him since before daybreak. It had been dark for some time, and we were coming back from a small community called Helicon. This was a particularly depressed area where you could pick up a pickup truck load of "colored hands" and work them from "kin til cain't" (from the time you *can* see until you *can't* see, i.e., daylight til dark). Uncle Vernon's wife, Aunt Faye, was driving the pickup truck and he and I were following her in their old blue '48 Mercury.

I was already thinking about Nappy's House (that's where Mother told us we went when we fell asleep) as we topped Finley Hill and passed the fire tower. Uncle Vernon had just steered the old car left onto the red dirt road that led back to the main house when sleep overtook him. Being as tired as I was, I thought at first I was seeing things as Uncle Vernon's chin hit his chest and we hit the ditch about twenty feet from the main highway.

Fortunately, we had had to slow down to make the turn and weren't going that fast. The abrupt stop shook Uncle Vernon from his slumber and, without a word, he threw the old buggy in reverse, eased her out of the ditch and back onto the road!

No damage was done, and I knew better than to say anything. It wasn't until I went to basic training at Ft. Campbell, Kentucky years later that I understood how someone could be so tired he could fall asleep somewhere besides in his bed.

LIFE LESSON NUMBER FORTY-TWO

Just because your eyes are open doesn't mean you're not asleep.

CHAPTER FORTY-THREE

My First Cattle "Drive"

My father just couldn't fathom the idea of being a farmer the rest of his life, so, after some "financial negotiations" with his parents and in-laws, he was able to come up with $1500 for The Triangle, a run-down combination gas station and grocery store about two miles north of town.

This was truly the forerunner of the modern-day convenience store, but with several advantages for customers. Without ever leaving the vehicle, a motorist could, with a smart toot of the horn, have an attendant (me, my sister, my mother, or my father) rush out, check the oil and water, put air in the tires, wash the windshield, and fill 'er up (with "regular" or "ethyl") quicker than he or she could turn off the ignition.

There were advantages for us as owners of this thriving business too, because we *lived* there, and could make a living by "waiting on customers" from the time our feet hit the floor in the morning until we laid our heads down at night. At least, our parents did; I spent most of my time "working to get out of work" in that confounded store. I did, however, learn to pump gas, wash windshields, and check oil at the tender age of about three and a half!

When kids back home grew up on the farm, it was sort of understood that, as soon as you shed your diapers, you learned how to drive. It made sense, because it was one less "hand" you had to hire to work, and, if you could drive one vehicle (truck, tractor, etc.), you could drive 'em all. Since my family moved off the farm when I was three, I didn't "officially" grow up on one, so I wasn't privy to the early childhood "drivers ed" the real farm kids got.

But my non-driving days came to a halt one summer day at the age of thirteen when I went back to the farm to visit. It was late afternoon, and Uncle Vernon and I were riding in his two-toned green International Harvester pickup. The old truck was loping over the clods in the pasture when suddenly Uncle Vernon realized he needed to be in two places at once. We were following a herd of cows when Uncle Vernon noticed a strategic gate was wide open. If the cows discovered it before we got there, it would be too late to stop them. Although I didn't understand any of the logistics of "cattle herding," something told me that time was of the essence. Vernon slammed on the brakes and shoved the transmission into neutral and, with the truck still rolling, jumped out and pointed.

"Drive the truck around that way! I'm gonna try to head 'em off before they get to the gate!"

His feet were already making time before I was able to stammer, "B…bu…but I don't know how to drive!"

I realized that this wouldn't have been a problem for a real farm boy, but the totality of my driving experience consisted of about ten minutes on Daddy's lap several years previously when he pretended to let me steer his car one night.

Time was a-wastin', and apparently, my inexperience presented no problem for Uncle Vernon, as he retorted, "You can't drive? Well, get under the wheel; I'll show you how!"

At least a precious ten seconds had elapsed from the time the open gate had been discovered, and I knew I needn't argue with Uncle Vernon. I figured I'd rather have a crash course (no pun intended) in driving than to chase cows all night.

So, with heart pounding and hands sweating, I slid behind the wheel. And a crash course it was! Uncle Vernon's frenetic instructions pounded my ears.

"See that? That's the gas. You mash that to go. But first, you put your left foot on that thing right there (he pointed to the clutch). Put it in gear (he quickly did that for me as I jammed the clutch to the floor), then let off on it as you mash the gas. Let's go!"

In a flash, he was gone, racing Bessie and her friends to the finish line. If I hadn't known better, I would have thought that I had some-how been hurled onto the back of one of those broncos as the truck lurched forward at breakneck speed. I hadn't heard anything akin to the word "slowly," which is how you're supposed to "let out" a clutch, and in the heat of the moment, my left foot came up as fast as it had gone down, but not quite as fast or as hard as my right foot hit the gas. My head hit the ceiling of the old truck as we went airborne!

None of that mattered right now, though, because, by golly, I was *driving!* And making darn good time too, by the way. In fact, so good that I almost made it to the gate before Uncle Vernon. Fortu-nately the cows had not a clue what was going on, and scattered in opposite directions as Uncle Vernon slammed the gate shut.

However, there was one small hitch. In his haste (an understate-ment), Uncle Vernon had forgotten to tell me how to stop. I'm sure I had heard of a brake, but it didn't dawn on me that the old truck even had one, let alone, where the pedal was or how to use it. Since my hands were already glued to the steering wheel, I held on tight, and called on some South Alabama Einstein logic. *Maybe if you mash it to make it go, if you don't mash it, maybe it'll stop.*

Fortunately, the truck wasn't aimed at anything but the open range as it galloped the last few yards and finally gave up the ghost in a cloud of smoke and dust. Although doubled over in laughter, some-how Uncle Vernon made it to the "driver's" side of the truck.

"Boy, you really can't drive, can you?" Uncle Vernon laughed.

"I told you I couldn't," I whimpered.

"Well, let's do it some more!" Uncle Vernon announced.

I spent the rest of that evening driving around that pasture, with Uncle Vernon patiently coaching me in the rudiments of the road—including how to "put on the brakes!"

Several months later, our parents bought my sister and me a flashy new (actually, it was used, but new to us!) 1953 Bel Air Chevro-let. Although it had three forward gears "on the column," I rarely got it out of first gear for the first several months as I drove ruts around The Triangle practicing for my driver's test which I took three years later in that very car.

The epilogue to this story is that, in our little town, the driver's test was given only on Wednesdays, and never when it was raining. In those days and in our school, we didn't have "learner's permits" or driver's ed; you just somehow learned how to drive and took the test and hoped to pass. I was the second youngest person in my high school class, so when I finally turned 16 in 1960, I was practically the only one without a driver's license.

You guessed it. I turned 16 on a Wednesday (couldn't sleep all night the night before), and woke up with the skies raining cats and dogs. As I dejectedly went to school that morning, I was counting the hours until the next Wednesday, when suddenly the clouds broke.

As prearranged, Daddy came to the school and picked me up (it was about 9 A.M.) and took me down to the courthouse where I passed the test with flying colors, thanks to my "driver's ed teacher," Uncle Vernon, a runaway herd of cows, and a *very tough* International Harvester truck.

LIFE LESSON NUMBER FORTY-THREE

Sometimes it's not where you're going, but knowing how to stop when you get there, that's important.

CHAPTER FORTY-FOUR

Lou Ellen Gets "Shot"

I have worn many "hats" in my lifetime, both vocationally and recreationally. I have also felt many emotions, both highs and lows. But, even as an adult, there is one thing that I have rarely felt, and that is bored.

Maybe it's because, growing up, my mother was always working and my father was both physically and emotionally distant. This sometimes forced me to find ways to entertain myself, even when friends were not around. Although there is some validity to the adage, "An idle mind is the devil's workshop," I believe there's an up side to an idle mind. It can also be fertile ground for creativity.

Left alone, I found that the most unlikely item would inspire me to "do something with it," or "make something out of it." Some of this creativity may have had its genesis in my first memory of carpenters sawing and nailing and building in my back yard. I became intrigued at how they could start with a board or plank, and end up with something totally unlike the original item. Later on, I was an avid fan of "Mr. Wizard," and was always trying out the experiments he showed on TV. I also had somewhat of a talent for art, and spent a lot of time drawing and sketching anything from cartoons and still life to people and animals.

I'm not sure where I learned the craft of dart making (I don't believe the idea was original), but once I started, I was always amazed at how quickly I could turn out those little missiles. I stress *little* because these were not Olympic-sized projectiles. In fact, their uniqueness was in their small size and simplicity.

The parts consisted of a wooden match stem, a needle from my mother's sewing kit, and the small paper liner from a tin of Bayer aspirin. The tools needed were either a pocket knife or a single edge razor blade and a pair of scissors. The head of the match was cut off and discarded, and the "eye" of the needle was inserted into the end of the match stem with the pointed end of the needle forming the "business end" of the dart. Two quarter-inch wide strips were cut from the aspirin box liner and inserted into a slot cut into the other end of the match stem. These strips were then bent open to form the "fins" that guided the missile. The manufacturing procedure took only about two to three minutes, and the finished product was a tiny lance which could be thrown with amazing accuracy (with a little practice, of course).

After a particularly productive morning of missile making, I was looking for new and exciting ways to show off my dart-throwing prowess.

Enter Lou Ellen Braxton. Lou Ellen was a rather attractive, tall, slender, red-haired, freckle-faced girl who was a little older than my sister, Jean. I had become friends with Lou Ellen's younger brother, Byron, and was always trying to impress her in one way or another.

I was back in my room at the rear of The Triangle when I heard Lou Ellen come in. I decided right then that I needed to show her what an expert marksman I was, so I gathered a small handful of darts and tip-toed to the door.

Lou Ellen was standing in front of the "meat case," happily chatting with Mother as I took aim. My purpose, of course, was not to hit Lou Ellen, but to land the little missile in the wooden floor right next to her left foot. If she was unfortunate enough to miss the "throw" itself, then I planned to triumphantly announce to her what I had just done. In my mind's eye, I could see the projectile finding its mark precisely inches from Lou Ellen's foot, and then her clapping with glee and oohing and aahing about what a smart little boy I was.

Although I had never attempted a shot this daring before—the distance from launch to target was a good 15 to 18 feet—I was certain I could pull it off. Unfortunately, I was not the William Tell I thought I was on that fateful morning. My aim was perfect, but the thrust was a mite too adequate, and, to my horror, the needle found its mark about three inches above Lou Ellen's left ankle bone. In order to make the distance, I had had to exaggerate the arc of the trajectory, and, to my amazement, the little dart stuck in Lou Ellen's bare leg at about a 65-degree angle, so slightly that she was unaware she had been "shot."

Well, suddenly I had a dilemma. My "processing" of the situation entered warp speed, while my legs went into slow-mo. *Should I run? Should I confess? Should I make up a lie? (What lie would cover this?!) Should I ignore what just happened? How could my life have fallen apart so quickly?*

I could hear Lou Ellen's and my mother's voices at what sounded like a 78 record playing at 33 and a third speed as I stepped through the door, drawn to the scene of the crime. It didn't help that Lou Ellen was so tall, and I felt like little David must have felt approaching Goliath. As I entered her majesty's presence, Lou Ellen slowly looked down, confused at the constipated look on my face.

"Oh, hi, Mike...what's wrong?" she asked.

I managed to feebly point to the point of entry and stammer, "Well, I, uh...that...it...you..."

It took Lou Ellen a nanosecond to spy the protruding projectile. The blood-curdling scream was heard all the way to town, and Lou Ellen's dance was a sight to behold!

Her jitterbug loosened the already precarious missile and hurled it skyward. I never found the little thing because, frankly, I was *outta there*, leaving poor Lou Ellen to lick her wound and my mother to try to figure out what the H*** had just happened.

Needless to say, I later suffered the consequences of my foolishness, and, to this day, a spirited game of darts is my least favorite "sport."

LIFE LESSON NUMBER FORTY-FOUR

If you're trying to impress a girl, throw <u>yourself</u> at her feet. . .not darts.

CHAPTER FORTY-FIVE

Attack Of The "Killer Bees"

Every summer at The Triangle, certain strange events would occur like clock work, and came to be expected as "normal." One of those phenomena was the annual convoy of "bee trucks."

I never knew where they came from, or where they were going. All I knew was that, once in a while, one or two of those insect-laden vessels would stop by for fuel. These trucks came to be seen as nothing to get particularly excited or concerned about, although, invariably, there would be the occasional small swarm of maverick bees that escaped the hives and relentlessly followed the convoy "on the wing." That is, until the day one of the queens escaped and proceeded to set up house on a nearby road sign in front of The Triangle, complete with her entourage of thousands of angry workers.

Part of my "job" growing up in a Mom and Pop country store was to pump gas, which I did from the time I could reach up and unscrew the gas cap. In those days, there was no such thing as "self-service." In fact, the thought of a customer even so much as *touching* a gas pump nozzle would be tantamount to theft of property or assault.

It was probably about nine or ten o'clock on a Saturday morning (usually a busy time for gas pumping and bee trucks), and what I didn't know was that earlier that morning, we had been visited by a particularly heavy-laden bee truck that had left behind the aforementioned queen and her brood. Happily pumping, I was totally unaware of the ominous swarm until, out of nowhere, one of the little critters zoomed in and released his ire about an inch below my right eye. I scarcely had time to shout a well-chosen invective and swat the beast away, when his partner popped me on my left elbow.

My next memory was of racing north on Highway 331 toward opposing traffic, arms flailing, with an occasional backward glance to check the status of the pursuing hoard. I never measured the distance to Mr. Rusty Furr's house in the curve north of The Triangle, but I would bet the family farm it was a good quarter mile. If it had been an Olympic event, I'm sure I would have won the gold medal!

I don't know if that customer ever got his gas tank filled, but I still warily check out that road sign when I go back "down home."

LIFE LESSON NUMBER FORTY-FIVE

You don't have to take steroids to run fast.

CHAPTER FORTY-SIX

Coke Bottles In The Willow Tree

If you could describe a "typical little boy," I must have been close. BB guns, dogs, cats, birds, chickens, high top boots, cow licks, skinned knees, fishing, and climbing trees. The latter was one of my favorite things to do.

Unfortunately, my father saw trees as a nuisance, what with all the leaves and limbs they shed and all, and when one would "volunteer" in the yard and get at least a foot high, he would promptly whack it down. Now I liked trees, and, having never seen them from Daddy's vantage point, I decided early on to take it upon myself to populate our yard with trees. Although there were plenty in the neighboring pasture, there were virtually none on the plot of ground we called The Triangle when we moved there, so I knew my work was cut out for me.

I began to notice which trees grew fast, and which ones took longer. If I was going to plant trees all over the yard, I had to pick the ones that would grow *fast*. Although pecan trees were great for climbing and the nuts were great for making pies, putting in fudge, or just eating right out of the shell, I knew they were out of the question, because they took a lifetime to mature. I was tipped off as to their slow growth by Daddy, because he told me that the grove of pecan trees on my grandparents' farm had been planted by him and my grandfather when he was a little boy. They were acceptable climbing size by now, but I knew that Daddy was the ripe old age of about 29 and too old to climb them!

I studied some of the faster-growing varieties I'd seen in the woods and pasture near The Triangle—chinaberries, mimosas (aka palmettos), and willows, and noticed that you could make chinaberry trees grow bigger if you kept the "suckers" cut back. I guess the little shoots that sprouted next to the main trunk were called suckers because they sucked the nutrients from the main tree, thus keeping it from getting much bigger than the bush itself. So one day, without telling Daddy, I got a shovel and dug up a small "bush" of chinaberry trees across the road and got Mother to get an ax and help me split the roots into three parts. We knew we couldn't swing that ax with precision, so Mother just put the blade between the shoots and stomped on it until they broke apart into three bedraggled little sticks that I hoped would be the beginnings of a back yard jungle gym for me. Incredibly, they all lived to become trees, but didn't grow fast enough for me to climb. Mother must have told Daddy what I was doing because they mysteriously survived his notorious machete.

The tree that eventually became my favorite "climber" was a willow that volunteered in the northeast corner of the yard. I think what got it started was the septic tank. It was always overflowing and creating a terrible stench. But it also created a fertile spot for this willow tree which liked wet, low places. Another plus for that location was that Daddy couldn't get to it to whack it down, because, if he tried, he'd bog down in the stinky muck!

That spot was just the ticket for that little sprig, because it grew exponentially, and seemed to almost double in size weekly! It took a little while, but eventually I began to test the limbs, and before I knew it, I was seeing the world from a lofty vantage point high above The Triangle. Unlike the stockier and sturdier pecan trees I climbed on the farm, the willow was, well, willowy, and would sway with the breeze as each year I climbed higher and higher.

By the time I reached pre-adolescence, the old willow had seen a lot of mileage, serving alternately as target practice for BB guns and "daggers," a basketball goal holder, and a home-made swing for my friends and me. Times were never boring around The Triangle, because customers were always coming in, and *something* was always going on. And even if nothing of import was happening, my friends and I could always find plenty to do.

Like the day my buddy, James stopped by for a cold "soda water" (aka "Co-coler"). All the soft drink bottles in those days were "returnable," and if you didn't drink the Coca Cola, Pepsi, or Grapico on the premises, you paid a penny "deposit," which you got back when you returned the bottle. Many of our customers would just pay the deposit and keep two or three bottles on hand so that when they bought a "drink," they could trade the "empty" in for a fresh cold one.

We kept our stash of empty bottles outside so that when the "drink man" came to collect them to replace with full ones, it was easier to load them onto his truck. Besides, if kept inside, the sugary empties attracted roaches and other critters, as there was no such thing as "diet" colas back then.

Well, James had just finished his drink when I had a brilliant idea for some recreation and fun. At some point in time, I had studied about the laws of nature, including gravity, inertia, and the speed at which objects fall when dropped from on high. You guessed it. What better way to test the law of gravity than to drop a few empty Coke bottles from high atop the old willow? I wondered why I hadn't thought of it before.

But first, we had to get the bottles up in the tree, right? No problem, because my buddy, James, had a great arm for throwin', and I discovered that if he threw a bottle at just the right velocity, he could get it to levitate right in front of me. Then all I had to do was reach out and grab it. Simple.

My perch was in a handy fork in the uppermost branches near the very top of the tree, so I could wrap my legs around the fork and leave my arms free for catching. What a great way to spend an afternoon. Throwing Coke bottles at each other from the top of a willow tree and learning about science at the same time!

This little lesson went on for some time, and with each *throw, catch, and drop*, James and I became more and more daring, varying the height and range of each throw with reckless abandon. We had it almost down to a science (no pun intended)—*throw, catch, drop, throw, catch, drop*—when suddenly we got out of sync. I had just caught a nice throw from James, and before he realized I hadn't dropped it back down, he hurled another one skyward!

That's when the scene went into slow motion. As my eyes followed the approaching missile, several thoughts went through my mind. *I can't drop this one. What if they collide? I can't let James get one up on me* (another pun not intended). *He threw it; therefore, I have to catch it.*

So the decision was made. *Hold onto the bottle I already had with one hand, and catch the second one with my other hand.* Simple, right? *Wrong!*

I don't know if it was last minute panic on James' part when he let that second bottle go, or if his throwin' arm had just gotten tired. In any case, this one sped up between the branches about eighteen inches off course. The velocity was nearly perfect though, and as the bottle made it ascent, it stalled about an arm's length away. Anticipating the stall, I leaned forward, feeling the willow's branches follow my lead as tree swayed to greet bottle. My trembling right hand encircled its target, and, instinctively, I pulled the bottle in toward me and swayed backward as the two bottles met in a loud *crack*, shattering both of them.

Back to reality and normal speed. What had seconds before been two perfectly good Coke bottles were now showering shards of glass headed for the top of James' head. Fortunately, he was faster than the speed of gravity and high-tailed it out from there before the first piece hit the ground. I didn't know until I shakily climbed down that a tiny piece of glass had struck me in the throat and lodged just below my Adam's Apple. The bleeding was minimal, so my mother patched me up with a single band-aid. The wound healed quickly, and it wasn't until months later when the spot started itching and I scratched it that out popped what was left of the most unforgettable science lesson I ever learned!

LIFE LESSON NUMBER FORTY-SIX

What goes up, must come down...but not necessarily the same way it went up.

CHAPTER FORTY-SEVEN

Riding The Scooter To Brenda's House

As a child, I had lots of friends. In a small town of less than 2,500, everybody knows everybody—and their business. But as far as I was concerned, socio-economic status meant nothing. If we "clicked" as friends, that's all I cared about. Although I'm sure my parents knew, I didn't know, or care, that I was not as "well off" as some of my friends, and "better off" than others. I do remember that there were certain kids who didn't seem to want to "associate" with the likes of me and my family. I wasn't really bothered by it; I just found it curious because I couldn't understand why anybody wouldn't want to have as many friends as possible.

There was one kid who was an exception to the rule. His name was Sammy, and he was one of the most popular boys in school. In my mind, he had *everything*. He came from "good stock"; his grandfather was a doctor, and most of his relatives on both sides were successful business or professional people. Although he had a younger brother who was somewhat of a "pill," Sammy was always perfectly well-behaved, and all the other kids (boys and girls) emulated him. It was considered an honor to be friends with Sammy. In fact, they could have easily taken the idea for Ozzie and Harriet from Sammy and his family.

That's why people were shocked when Sammy's parents bought him a "motorbike." This was back when only hoodlums and Hell's Angels rode such things, and Hondas (cars *or* motorcycles) weren't even invented yet. Movie stars such as James Dean hadn't helped the image of bikers during that time either.

But, as with anything else he touched, Sammy made "motor biking" respectable—at least in our little town—and pretty soon the other parents accepted Sammy's putt-putt as just another mode of transportation. You weren't required to have a license, or wear a helmet, to drive a motorcycle back then. It was sort of understood that, if you could ride a bicycle, you could drive a motorcycle.

I had always been a lover of bicycles because it was the vehicle that first gave me *freedom*. When things started to get dull for me, or work seemed imminent, I could go fishing, exploring, or just escape on my trusty two-wheeled steed.

But when Sammy got his motorbike, I began pressuring my parents for one too. Basically, I tended to be lazy, and pedaling seemed to be too much of a chore after seeing Sammy's motorized wonder. I guess the previous propaganda had worked on my parents, though, because they wouldn't hear of it. The excuses were always the same. "They're too dangerous," or "You might get hurt," or "You don't need one of those things; you've got a bicycle." The battle raged for years, but my parents were absolutely uncompromising on the issue. Nevertheless, my obsession with "motorized bicycles" grew, and I vowed that someday I would own, or, at least, ride one.

That opportunity came one day when my buddy, James, showed up on his "scooter." I knew something was going on when he came into the store all dirtied up from head to toe. James' family didn't have much money, but they "made do" with what they had. His father was a carpenter and could build just about anything. His older brother was pretty cool too; he was always giving James "junk stuff" which he, in turn, shared with me.

"Come here, Mike, let me show you something," he said with a wide grin.

"What is it?" I responded.

"It's a motor scooter," he replied excitedly. "You wanna go for a ride?"

So, it had come to this. Suddenly my big chance to ride a motorized bicycle presented itself in this bucket of bolts on wheels. "Well, yeh, where we goin'?" I asked.

"I don't know. Wherever you wanna go!"

I couldn't believe my ears (or eyes!). The freedom of the open road was calling me! For the first time in my life, I could ride away without those apron strings! I could go farther and faster than I'd ever gone before!

"Let's go to Brenda's house!" I shouted.

Brenda was a friend of my sister's and I knew she had just gone over there. Brenda was a cute 17 year old, and the kind of girl any young boy just *wanted* to impress. Brenda usually only noticed me if I was with my sister, and even then, she merely tolerated me.

What a golden opportunity! Now I could prove to this hot chick how special and tough and desirable I was. But then James dropped a bomb.

"There's just one problem," he said. "This scooter ain't got a starter. If you want to ride with me, I gotta push it off, and then you gotta jump on it when I come by."

Well, it never dawned on me that James didn't have more than about thirty minutes of riding experience. I'd never seen him on one before, but he seemed so confident, so I figured, why not?

There was another problem, however. I knew if I asked my mother if I could ride this contraption with James over to Brenda's house—or anywhere for that matter—the answer would be a re-sounding *"No way!"*

I don't know what got into me. Usually a very compliant young boy, I struggled for only about two seconds before motioning for James to *bring it on!* If they'd had video cameras back then, I'm sure we would've won the grand prize on America's Funniest Home Videos, as James pushed that scooter to the top of the hill, with both of us in anticipation of the ride of our lives.

"Get ready!" hollered James. "Here I come!"

With about three giant steps to overcome inertia, James mount-ed the rusty rattletrap with Roy Rogers skill and careened toward me at the blinding speed of about five miles an hour. Of course, it seemed much faster as I grabbed hold of James' shoulders and flung my leg over the seat.

We have liftoff! Wrong direction! Banking on the loose gravel, we made a hasty U-turn and chugged back up the hill toward Brenda's house. Lurching and belching smoke, the scooter somehow made it the twenty feet or so to Highway 10 and away we went!

Who can describe the thrill of their first motorcycle ride? It wasn't exactly what I had envisioned, but, hey, beggars can't be choosers, right?

Cars were already backing up behind us as we "burned up" Highway 10 at an unbelievable speed of 20-25 miles an hour. And whoever heard of mufflers? Even at that speed, the noise was deafening as we made our ascent up the final hill to Brenda's house.

This presented several more challenges, however. Until now, we hadn't given much thought to Brenda's house being on the left side of the road, which meant we had to *cross* traffic. Also, Brenda's driveway wasn't visible from the road, as it was bordered by two large red dirt banks. Plus, we were headed west *at sundown*, and the sun was blazing just above the horizon at the crest of the hill we were driving up. And the final nail in the coffin (bad choice of words), our bucket of bolts might not have been much in the way of amenities, but it did have a huge, oversized windshield, complete with years of scratches and cracks!

Yet, I trusted James to deliver us safely to Brenda's door. Forget blinkers! Forget hand signals! We were holding on for dear life (literally!) as James banked left (another bad choice of words) and eased across the other lane—about ten feet short of the driveway.

It's funny how sometimes we block out unpleasant memories—especially *embarrassing* unpleasant memories. I do remember the taste of red dirt in my mouth, however, and the large black spot in my vision from the blinding sun as we pulled our bruised, but otherwise unbroken bodies out of that ditch.

Don't ask me what happened next. I'm sure Brenda and my sister came out and saw the pitiful sight—a far cry from the impression I had wanted to make. I believe we managed to push the scooter back down the hill and back to The Triangle where my mother, I'm sure, confirmed to me her belief that motorcycles were the most dangerous things since rattlesnakes.

I never saw that scooter after that day. It just sort of "disappeared" and became one of those things that was never discussed again. Amazingly though, I did become somewhat of a motorcycle enthusiast, and have owned eight of them since then. But because I knew she would worry that I might get hurt, I never let my mother know I owned a single one of those infernal "motorized bicycles."

LIFE LESSON NUMBER FORTY-SEVEN

If you're trying to impress a girl, don't let the stars (or the sun!) get in your eyes.

CHAPTER FORTY-EIGHT

David Builds A Ping Pong Table

I've always believed that a boy needs a father figure to look up to. If he doesn't have one naturally, he'll find one somewhere. It might be a teacher, another family member, or even an older "gang" member. If he doesn't make that connection, he'll spend a good part of his adult life trying to figure out what manhood is all about.

I was fortunate to have more than one father figure who were great influences in my growing up years. Although my father did the best he could, he had his own agenda and his own personal demons he was battling during some of those years. A teacher once told me that she had heard how one father apologized to his son by stating, "Son, I'm sorry I wasn't there for you, but I wasn't there for me, either." I took solace in that, believing that is exactly what my father would have said, had he known how. Later on, when he "laid down the bottle," we made up for some of that time we had lost.

In the meantime, my maternal uncle, "Doc," and my paternal uncle, Vernon, filled in, and those times were unforgettable. Family took care of family, we believed, and they did it well.

One day, though, an unexpected father figure showed up at our door. His name was David, and he needed a place to live while the road crew he was working with was resurfacing Highway 331 near The Triangle. He said he didn't know how long he'd need the place; it would depend on the weather and how smoothly the project went. Mother told him we didn't have any rooms, but we did have an attic. We could fix him a bed, and he could stay up there. David accepted the terms, and thus began our bonding with David.

If there is a "typical" construction worker, David would've come close. He was rather good-looking, thin and muscular, with swarthy, sun-cured skin from years of outside work. His teeth were few, and not in very good shape. Not much time to brush when you're building roads, he would say. He was also a heavy smoker, a habit picked up years earlier when nobody was there to stop him. We never knew very much about him, but as strange as it seems now, David became a part of our family, sometimes having meals with us, helping around the store, and slowly building a relationship with my sister and me.

Not surprisingly, David was good at "making" things, and would often be our handyman when something needed repairing. One day Jean and I decided we wanted to play ping pong. We later learned it was sometimes called table tennis. I guess we had heard about the game from some of our friends, and it looked sort of like a smaller version of regular tennis, which we had seen our neighbors across the road playing. We thought they were rich because they had their own asphalt tennis court nestled in a big shady pecan grove.

So, we raided our stash of junk for some materials to get started, and hit up David for assistance. He told us he'd never built a ping pong table, so we told him what we thought it ought to look like. Jean and I had already conned our mother into buying us the net, paddles, and balls at the "Ten Cent Store," and when David finished, we had the only custom built table tennis table in town!

Of course, we didn't have a garage or carport to put it in (much less a game room), so it stayed right where it was built, and, in a couple of hours, we were chasing ping pong balls all over the back yard! We soon discovered, however, some of the drawbacks of using scrap materials to build a ping pong table. David did a great job, and we really appreciated his efforts, but, well, for one thing, he didn't use finishing nails to nail the plywood together for the table top. So, every time a ball would hit one of those nail heads—*ding!*—it would fire off in an unexpected direction, leaving the receiver of the serve scratching his or her head.

Fortunately, it didn't rain for the first several days, and the "tournaments" went well. But after the first big rain, we discovered that scrap plywood nailed together in pieces warps when it gets wet.

It would usually take two or three days for it to dry out and get flat again. It never would reach its original state, though, and eventually we had to dismantle it, thus dashing our dreams of being pro table tennis players.

Years later, when the Nixon administration initiated "ping pong diplomacy" with the Red Chinese, I remember wondering if either team would have fared as well if they'd had David's old home made ping pong table to play on!

Before its demise, David's old table saw many a "contest," and gave us an opportunity to learn a sport we would never have been exposed to otherwise. It was sort of like David himself. Once the table had served its purpose, it was gone.

Almost as suddenly as he had showed up at our door, one day David was gone. After a quick and tearful goodbye, we never saw him again. I guess the grown ups thought it would be better that way. We never "processed" his departure from our lives. It was just accepted that that chapter was over and it was time to move on.

It is said that time heals all wounds, and so it was with David. Occasionally I'll be reminded of him and remember the good times we shared. Many years after I saw David for the last time, I had the privilege of becoming friends with a woman named Judith. We had attended classes together, working toward our Master's degrees, and subsequently worked together briefly. She and her husband moved to Pennsylvania after his retirement from the Air Force, but only after Judith and I had developed a strong professional and personal bond.

Judith gave me a copy of a poem she had acquired that summed up our relationship. I have shared it with many people since. It reminded me of the relationship David and I had, and reads as follows:

It seems wherever I go
People come into my life or go out of it
Touching me where I can feel
Then leaving me only a memory
Like the gossamer fairy tales of children—
Leaving me,

And I wasn't finished knowing them.

How do I know
Who I am seeing for the last time?
How do you halt your life to gather and keep those
around you
That you've ever known?
And how do you keep fairy tales from losing their
magic?

So come
Brush against the walls of my life
And stay long enough for us to know each other
Even though we'll have to part sometime
And we both know
The longer you stay
The more I'll want you back when you are gone.

But come anyway
For fairy tales are the happiest stories we read
And great books are made of little chapters.
. . .Author Unknown

LIFE LESSON NUMBER FORTY-EIGHT

A true friend reaches for your hand...and touches your heart.

CHAPTER FORTY-NINE

The Roots Of My Raisin'

As far back as I can remember, there was an emphasis on religion in our family. We were all considered Christians, but doctrinally, my father's side of the family were mostly Methodists, and my mother's side were mostly Baptists. Regardless of doctrine, they were all very conservative and traditional.

My paternal grandmother Annie's favorite preacher was Oral Roberts. She listened to his "healing crusades" faithfully for years on radio. She believed in the power of prayer, and truly believed the reason she was never healed of crippling arthritis was because she didn't have enough "faith." I overheard her praying one day toward the end of her life, "Lord, I know you're ready for me, but I'm not quite ready to go yet."

None of the women on that side of the family believed in cutting their hair. In fact, it was considered a sin to do so. They believed this admonition came from the book of I Corinthians, Chapter 11, Verses 13, 14, and 15, which reads: *Judge in yourselves: is it comely that a woman pray unto God uncovered? Doth not even nature itself teach you, that, if a man have long hair, it is a shame unto him? But if a woman have long hair, it is a glory to her: for her hair is given her for a covering.* There was even a song we used to play on the Victrola called "Why Do You Bob Your Hair, Girls?" The words of the song were more intolerant than the scriptures. The words went something like this: *"Why do you bob your hair, girls? It is an awful shame. You rob the head God gave you, and wear the flapper's name. You're taking off your covering; it is an awful sin. Why do you bob your hair, girls? Short hair belongs to men!"* Nevertheless, this was considered an important tenet to follow, and my saintly paternal great aunt, Nina, kept her hair long and straight until her death at age 91.

It was also customary back then, when a couple got married, for the wife to change her church affiliation to whatever her husband's was. So when my mother married my father, she left her Hardshell Baptist background, and became a full-fledged Methodist. This was about as big a leap as one could take in the Protestant faith without jumping out of it. For example, Hardshell or Privative (we called it Primitive) Baptists believe, to the extreme, that "once you're saved, you're always saved," whereas Methodists believe you can "fall from grace" and lose your salvation by repeatedly and willfully sinning. Water is an important part of worship in the Hardshell Baptist church, and some of the more traditional churches still wash the feet of parishioners in their services as Christ did for his disciples. And, of course, total immersion in water at baptism is mandatory; otherwise it is not considered "valid." In contrast, the most water you'll see in a Methodist baptism is in the little bowl the preacher dips his hand into to sprinkle the convert.

My mother took all this in stride, and adjusted quite well, even teaching Sunday School for a time in our local Methodist church. And, although Daddy wasn't much of a church goer, Mother always required that Jean and I get up on Sunday morning and at least attend Sunday School. We rarely stayed for church because Mother was expected to have dinner (that's what we called lunch) ready by noon. Sometimes we would stay and Mother or Daddy would pick us up later. We considered church an integral part of our lives growing up. When we did attend on Sunday night as a family, it was always a special time of closeness for us.

But then, one day, "scandal" rocked our family to the core. Jean's good friend, Nonie, had been a life long member of the Baptist church, and frequently invited my sister to go with her. One Easter Sunday, Jean came home after attending church with Nonie and announced that she had joined the Baptist church and been baptized!

This was an unspeakable break with tradition, and totally unacceptable. The shock soon wore off, however, and we all adjusted to the fact that we had a reprobate in the family, and that, from this point on, we would be "split up" on Sundays. Fortunately, in our little town, the Methodist and Baptist churches were right around the corner from each other, so logistically, it wasn't much of a problem. And, since most all of our friends at school were Methodists or Baptists, we felt at home in either church.

I remained loyal to Methodism and "officially" joined the church at age of ten or eleven after struggling for some time with the issue of salvation. Most of my friends had already joined the church and were urging me to do the same. I held back for what I thought were two good reasons. Having never learned to swim, I wasn't very comfortable with the idea of being dunked underwater in front of an audience. I was relieved when I finally got documented proof that Methodists only sprinkle, and that I had nothing to fear. But my biggest fear was that I wasn't really "saved," and I wanted to make sure I wasn't lying to God when I answered those questions the preacher asks right before you get baptized.

So I waited several weeks and pondered my future with the church, finally taking solace in the scriptural admonition to "work out your own salvation with fear and trembling" (Philippians 2:12). After much thought and prayer, I accepted Christ as my savior and was sprinkled shortly thereafter to make it "official."

I was still not sure about the total immersion thing, and was afraid I had copped out by just being sprinkled, so, many years later, just to be *sure*, I was baptized again (i.e., immersed) by a Nazarene preacher in the Cahaba River near Birmingham, during the time my family and I were living and worshiping there.

LIFE LESSON NUMBER FORTY-NINE

Sometimes, you have to know where you've come from to know where you're going.

CHAPTER FIFTY

Mules Are Forever

I have been privileged to live in an era that has seen tremendous change and progress in every area of our lives. Well over a half century of memories cram my brain: the invention of the ball point pen, landing on the moon, using a hand-crank telephone, the advent of FM radio, a young Roy Rogers growing old and dying, and the end of the Berlin Wall, just to name a few.

Although the title of this book is partly metaphorical, it brings back memories of ol' Ed and his big gray horse tied to a post in the corner of our yard; the old man in the Sears & Roebuck wagon with his mule clopping down the highway, almost oblivious to the speeding cars passing him by; my grandfathers, uncles and aunts plowing the fields with their trusty old mules.

A mule is defined as "the offspring of a donkey and a horse; especially, the offspring of a jackass and a mare." Although usually sterile and incapable of reproduction, they were bred because they were tough, stubborn, and long-lasting.

Although it's only about an hour's drive away, I rarely get down to the "old home place" anymore. (That's what I, and most of my southern compatriots, call that hallowed piece of ground where "the old folks" used to live.) There's not much there for me, except those tough, stubborn, long-lasting memories. When I began to see the end of this book approaching, I recently made a trip back there to see if it would conjure up anything that I might want to include in its final pages.

As I pulled into the overhang where countless customers parked and bought gas or ran in for a quick loaf of bread, I felt a rush of emotions. The gas pumps were gone, and the store was boarded up. As I peered through the griminess of old glass on the front door, I flashed back through decades of history, and momentarily watched the movie of time as it fast forwarded back to the present. Looking up, I saw the eye bolts still fastened to the large wooden beams which served as supports for the swings my sister and I enjoyed on hot summer days. I heard the laughter, smelled the smells, saw the images, and felt the exhilaration of being young and full of promise.

Most of the surrounding buildings are gone now, where "Miss Alma," "Miss Clara," and "Mr. William," and others in the neighborhood lived. As I made my way to the rear of The Triangle, I saw that one of the buildings across the road was now a store of some kind. Looking closer through tear-filled eyes, I could see the sign above the door. It read: *BIG DADDY'S OUTDOORS.*

I thought how appropriate it was that the owners of that building had unknowingly honored the memory of my father and his family's contribution to that little corner of the world. And for a split second I thought I saw those *"mules in the fast lane"* once again.

LIFE LESSON NUMBER FIFTY

It takes tough things in life to make a gentle-man.

GLOSSARY

When I first got the idea to put some of my stories down on paper and make a book out of them, I started by simply making a list. After several days of "rewinding my camcorder," I ended up with eight pages or so of "titles" of outstanding things, people, and events which I added to and subtracted from as I journeyed back in time. I then loosely divided these into categories such as "school," "farm," "religion," "Triangle," etc.

There have been times when I would encounter situations which would often trigger a memory long since tucked away in my sub-conscious—either a word, a phrase, or an entire experience I hadn't thought about in years. Many of these can be traced back to the farm or rural background I grew up in, so I thought it would be helpful to include a glossary of significant terms and phrases.

Most of the following definitions will probably not be found in any of today's dictionaries. The list is, by no means, all inclusive, but merely a compilation of the more "popular" key words and phrases that were commonly used during the time I was growing up. Where appropriate, some may be used in a sentence for clarification.

Bitter weed—A weed usually found in pastures that makes pretty yellow flowers and is capable of taking over the whole pasture. It is bitter to livestock, so farmers don't like it.

"Book" bacon—Redneck term for bulk—or unsliced—bacon; usually found in "country" stores. Many people swear it tastes better than pre-sliced or pre-packaged bacon.

"Book" baloney—Redneck term for bulk—or unsliced—bologna; usually found in "country" stores. Many people swear it tastes better than pre-sliced or pre-packaged bologna.

Bullace—A purple first cousin to the scuppernong. (See scuppernong.)

Chimley—Mispronunciation of "chimney." What Santa Claus is supposed to come down on Christmas Eve night.

China Berry—A fast-growing tree (sometimes a bush if you don't trim it right) that makes green (inedible, i.e., uneatable) berries. Its blossoms smell very sweet in the spring, but the rotting berries make a big mess in the fall.

Cons—Pecans; nuts that grow on big, good-climbing trees. Yankees call them "pee-cans." *"I'd sure like some of that 'con pie."*

Corn crib—A small shed, usually wooden, with a tin roof used for storing dried corn during the winter. A popular haven for rats and a variety of other rodents.

Cuckle burr—A bigger version of a sand spur. (See sand spur.) Some non-southerners pronounce it and spell it "cocklebur." The inspiration for today's Velcro.

Dinner—Meal eaten in the middle of the day; usually the second meal of the day. Some non-southerners think this is the third meal of the day, i.e., the meal eaten at night. They also sometimes call this "lunch."

Dog fennel—A green pungent fast-growing perennial weed that can take over a pasture. Cows don't like it and it's not good for anything.

Go out—Use the rest room (not necessarily the outhouse). It's an old-timey term and rarely used today. *"Have you got to go out?"*

Hands—"Hired help" or employees, usually hired by the day to work for kin til cain't.

Hockey—Go to the bathroom; "number 2."

Iron weed—A tough green weed sometimes used by young boys to prove they were men—if they could pull it up by the roots (which was impossible).

Kin til cain't—Daylight til dark; i.e., from the time you *can* see until you *can't* see. *"We gonna work you boys from kin til cain't."*

May case—Make haste; hurry up. Usually uttered by grandparents and directed toward kids when they were ready to go somewhere and kids were dilly-dallying or lolly-gagging.

May Pop—A vine that grows on the side of the road and makes a green fruit about the size of a lemon that looks like a tiny Stone Mountain watermelon. It starts growing good around May, and when you step on it, it "pops." Hence, the name. Its flower is beautiful, lacy, purple, and delicate. (See passion flower in a regular dictionary.)

Mule—The offspring of a donkey and a horse; especially, the offspring of a jackass and a mare. Although usually sterile and incapable of reproduction, they were bred because they were tough, stubborn, and long-lasting.

Nappy's house—Where you go when you fall asleep; often used as a warning to get into bed. *"Come on; it's time to go to Nappy's house."*

Nettle—A sticker that hurts like H*** if you touch it or rub up against it.

Pie safe—A "kitchen cabinet", usually equipped with a flour sifter for making biscuits, and storage compartments for pies, cakes, and other goodies.

Possum—A stinky, ugly rat-like animal about the size of a big cat that you have to hold your nose to eat. Best if eaten with potatoes. The dish is commonly called "possum and 'taters." Some people spell it with an "O" in front of it.

Rabbit tobacco—A weed that often grows in pastures. In the spring it has a sort of red color, but turns dark brown in the fall. Cows don't like it, but some farm boys claimed they smoked it.

Road scraper—A big (usually yellow) machine with a big sharp blade under it used for "scraping" country roads smooth. They usually appeared a few days after a big rain when the roads had dried them out, leaving deep ruts.

Rollin' store—A panel truck with shelves inside stocked with a lot of good things to buy really cheap. Sometimes it would come by right after the road scraper.

Sand spur—A sticker; a plant that produces stickers (as seeds). This particular seed (or sticker) comes off the plant and sticks to almost anything that rubs up against it. If it ever comes up in your yard, you can't get rid of it.

Scupnun—"Country" name for scuppernong; a grape-like fruit that grows on vines, sometimes wild, sometimes not. You don't eat it; you just suck the juice out and spit the rest of it out. Sometimes used for making juice, jelly...or wine.

Step ins—Little girls' panties.

Sticker—A weed with thorns.

Supper—The last meal of the day, usually eaten at night.

Ten Cent Store—A "variety" store where most everything used to cost ten cents. Some people used to call it the "Five and Dime."

Toboggan—A cap (usually knitted) worn in the winter. It can be pulled down over the ears, and eyes, if necessary.

Tread salve—A type of sticker that produces green "berries" that look like chinaberries. This spelling cannot be confirmed.

23579897R00189

Made in the USA
Columbia, SC
13 August 2018